PUNK ROCK WOMEN ALIVE AND WELL IN SOUTH PHILLY

Anne Cecil

PUNK ROCK WOMEN ALIVE AND WELL IN SOUTH PHILLY

Friends Are the Family You Choose

The Fashion and Personal Style Studies Collection

Collection Editor

Joseph H. Hancock II

This book is for my South Philly Punk family – youse all know who youse are.

First published in 2024 by Lived Places Publishing

All rights reserved. No part of this publication may be reproduced, stored in a retrieval system, or transmitted in any form or by any means, electronic, mechanical, photocopying, recording or otherwise, without prior permission in writing from the publisher.

The authors and editors have made every effort to ensure the accuracy of information contained in this publication, but assume no responsibility for any errors, inaccuracies, inconsistencies and omissions. Likewise, every effort has been made to contact copyright holders. If any copyright material has been reproduced unwittingly and without permission the Publisher will gladly receive information enabling them to rectify any error or omission in subsequent editions.

Copyright © 2024 Lived Places Publishing

British Library Cataloguing in Publication Data
A CIP record for this book is available from the British Library

ISBN: 9781916985032 (pbk)
ISBN: 9781916985056 (ePDF)
ISBN: 9781916985049 (ePUB)

The right of Anne Cecil to be identified as the Author of this work has been asserted by them in accordance with the Copyright, Design and Patents Act 1988.

Cover design by Fiachra McCarthy
Book design by Rachel Trolove of Twin Trail Design
Typeset by Newgen Publishing UK

Lived Places Publishing
Long Island
New York 11789

www.livedplacespublishing.com

Abstract

Say the word "punk" to anyone and their first thought is likely to be a man with a painted and studded motorcycle jacket and a mohawk. This is the stereotypical London Punk still sitting on the locks in Camden Town today charging tourists for a photo. Historically and even today, Punk Culture has been viewed as a masculine and "in your face" youth subculture with little room for the inclusion of girls. In fact, Punk is a highly localized culture that reflects place through sound, aesthetics, fashion, styles, mores, and ethos.

While Punk ideology certainly allows for gender equality, many of the scenes and much of the subcultural theory surrounding Punk have ignored the contribution and participation of women. My personal experience of the Philly scene is quite different. Women have been and continue to be important players, fully participating as creators and cultural producers, community and infrastructure builders, and institutional developers.

Keywords

Punk Culture, Punk Rock, Punk Revival, Punk Style, Punk Music, DIY Ethic, Philadelphia Underground Music Scene

Acknowledgments

This memoir reflects a collective effort on the part of my South Philly Punk family, who supported, encouraged, and inspired me generously in ways for which I am forever grateful and appreciative. Your insightful conversations and thoughtful responses to my survey have been invaluable. This journey would not have been possible without each one of you. I am profoundly thankful for your continuous support and inspiration.

Language

I have made an intentional choice to identify respondents to my survey as follows: Respondent #... Except for Marina D'Angelo, who agreed to be profiled for this book, I have referred to the band members of KeN by their band names.

Contents

Warning – PUNK is a four-letter word		x
Introduction		xi
Learning objectives		xiii
Preface: My Punk autobiography		xiv
Chapter 1	Debunking academic Punk: How I punked the academy	1
Chapter 2	What Punk is: What Punk is not	9
Chapter 3	It's a Philly thing: Badass things happen in Philly	17
Chapter 4	Philly Punk music: "So much fun, I love KeN" profile: Marina D'Angelo, cofounder, KeN the band	47
Chapter 5	A celebration of failure, innovation, and success profile: Judith Schaechter, international stained glass artist	57
Chapter 6	Eat more veggies profile: Elizabeth Fiend, Change Agent	65
Chapter 7	"We are we": A reflection	75
Chapter 8	Teaching Punk Culture	89
Explore Punk Culture activities		95
References		97
Recommended further reading		103
Index		105

Warning – PUNK is a four-letter word

This book contains content that reflects the historical and cultural context in which it was lived. Some language, depictions, and viewpoints may be considered offensive, inappropriate, or outdated by today's standards. These elements are preserved to provide an accurate representation of the era and to facilitate critical discussion and understanding of the past. Reader discretion is advised.

Please be aware Punk messaging across all media is intentionally shocking and offensive due to its criticism of societal norms and provocative themes. It is deliberately designed to make the content consumer uncomfortable. References to potentially offensive topics occur **frequently** and **throughout the book**. Be prepared to be offended.

Introduction

This book is a memoir, a historical account of my personal history based on my personal knowledge with help from some special sources. It began as a series of conference papers and presentations, but from the beginning it was intended to be a book. I explore and recount the development and maturation of Punk Culture and women's roles in the movement in South Philly from the late 1980s to today. The research includes a 2007 survey; one-on-one interviews conducted in 2010, 2023, and 2024; an ethnographic study; and autobiographical anecdotes.

While many women (and men) have contributed to the book, three women are profiled to provide examples of various Punk tenets in practice:

- Elizabeth Fiend, Change Agent and Activist who has spent her life promoting good health, environmentalism, and community activism through a bricolage of activities;
- Judith Schaechter, a renowned Stained Glass Artist and educator whose DIY (do it yourself) process brought innovation to the stained glass medium; and
- Marina D'Angelo, PhD, educator, and cofounder of the band KeN, a reaction to the traditional gender roles seen in Punk and rock bands.

Since the Reagan era, all of us women have used and continue to use empowerment, agency, and voice to move forward and react to the conventions of the time. Willing to try and not afraid to fail, we women continue to push boundaries and transform our lives and the world around us. It is primarily because we women have maintained those early relationships that we have transformed into the extended Punk family that we have become.

Learning objectives

1. Define subculture
2. Apply subculture to identity
3. Examine Punk Culture
4. Practice a Punk Identity
5. Develop a plan to incorporate the lessons learned from Punk practice into a critical analysis of the world

Preface: My Punk autobiography

I Am Punk, a script for a live performance presented at various events from 2008 - present

I never really thought of myself as the quintessential Punk. I had given up my pink Mohawk, ripped tights, leather jacket, and army boots ages ago – well, mostly. In July of 2005, I caught the IFC channel's documentary *Punk: Attitude*. The documentary ends with Henry Rollins, the lead singer of Black Flag, a band from Southern California that pioneered hardcore (a faster, harder, aggressive expression of punk rock), asking, "Why isn't everyone Angry?" And bang, it hit me – I am Punk.

I came of age in the late 70s, early 80s. I was deeply affected by world events – the Vietnam War, student protest, the student killing at Kent State (1970, the Ohio National Guard opened fire on unarmed college students protesting the Vietnam War, resulting in four deaths that raised serious questions about the use of military force against civilians, which became a rallying point for civil rights protesters), Bloody Sunday in Ireland (1972, British soldiers shot and killed 14 unarmed civil rights protesters), Watergate (1972, a break-in at the Democratic National Committee office that reshaped American politics and trust in government). These are ones that come to mind immediately and, given some time, I am sure I can name more. I was dreadfully bored with the hippie, free-love counterculture of my eldest sibling and the ego-stroking 20-minute jack-off rock ballad era of my second sibling. I was primed for the nihilist Punk perspective. While my older siblings chanted, "Never trust anyone over 40," I was screaming, "Never trust ANYONE in POWER!"

Don't get me wrong. There were some great artists before Punk – Janis (Joplin), Jimi (Hendrix), the (Rolling) Stones. In fact, the first song I ever knew all the words to was "Ruby Tuesday." The music of the era reflected the times. Punk was just the next expression and it belonged to me.

Punk transcended the music and fashion scene to become a mature culture. It has been portrayed as a masculine and aggressive movement, but this was never my experience of Punk. Masculine aggression is my definition of hardcore and that is a completely different animal.

I characterize myself as an original Punk or old-school Punk as defined by Lauraine LeBlanc in her book *Pretty in Punk* (1999). According to LeBlanc, original punks are Punks who have been into the scene since the late 1970s/early 1980s. They have a Punk fashion aesthetic that does not hold true to the stereotypical Punk style. They are employed in artistic fields and still have ties to their local music scene (1999, p. 60). This describes me and many of my Punk rock friends of nearly 40 years. Many are employed in education and the sciences as well as the arts, and most are active in local bands, political efforts, and/or independent film.

My personal Punk experience includes the following:

- Three key elements: bricolage, DIY (do it yourself), and transformation;
- One traditional value: family; and
- A heavy dose of sarcasm, parody, and satire as the most common form of personal expression.

This ideology plays out in all areas of my life.

Dictionary.com defines bricolage as follows:

1. A construction made of whatever materials are at hand; something created from a variety of available things;
2. (In literature) a piece created from diverse resources;
3. (In art) a piece of makeshift handiwork; and
4. the use of multiple, diverse research methods.

In my Punk life, bricolage can be applied to many facets: work, living space, personal style, artistic expression, even this book. My CV shows seven jobs, three businesses, 25 art shows, 17 conference presentations, 11 publications, and ten recognitions for various activities over 40 years. My home combines all sorts of items from numerous art/design styles and time periods. Most of my furnishings are hand-me-over, reuse, or recycled items. My personal style is usually classified as a "London" look, but I can wear anything from combat boots and studded leather to a corporate suit and perfectly look myself. My wardrobe includes new garments, thrift shop finds, vintage pieces, and items acquired through clothes swaps with my friends. My art is conceptual in that I select a theme or idea and then execute it in whatever media I feel is most appropriate to my message, with collage as the overreaching aesthetic. My academic research, even this project, includes a bricolage of methods and subjects.

So how did a privileged white woman live her life as the other?

Looking back, I was Punk before I was an embryo. I was born on August 12, 1962, to Henry and Pat. Pat was an immigrant from England. She was educated as a doctor in England during World War II. There were seats at university because most of the men were fighting. But when they returned, the men were given preferences for jobs, so off she came to the United States. She became one of the 4–6 percent of doctors who were women in 1960s America (Walling, Nilsen, and Templeton, 2020). As a child psychiatrist, she settled into a job where she met Henry. Henry was a pediatrician who was divorced, with custody of two young children. In the 1960s, the divorce rate was relatively low, around 22–24 percent (Our World in Data, 2018), and about 1 percent of fathers had sole custody of minor children (Pew Research Center, 2013). In Henry's case, it was because his wife was found to be unfit. Henry and Pat married in 1961 and I arrived on the scene one week shy of their one-year anniversary. In hindsight, Henry married Pat to fix his children, and Pat married Henry because she wanted a child. It took her until her early 30s to settle into her profession and she had me at 36. In the 1960s, that was considered old to have a first child.

A childhood of betwixt and between

From birth, I've been caught betwixt and between, half first-generation immigrant and half ninth-generation immigrant. Pat, as an immigrant, was already the other. The other mother.

The English woman. When I arrived, I became the other too. The daughter of the other mother. The daughter of the Englishwoman. The child with both her parents raising her. Henry cultivated this "otherness" from day one. It was he, my half-sister and half-brother on one side, and my mother and I on the other. I found myself betwixt and between them all, becoming the gatekeeper, facilitator, and negotiator from birth. There were all sorts of arguments about my half-brother and half-sister. There was always a different set of expectations for my half-brother and my half-sister than there was for me. I was held to a higher standard, while their standard was relaxed because they had been "traumatized" and supposedly I had not.

Really? I was one of the very few children of divorce in school, and divorce held a real stigma. It was off-putting and that created an air of secrecy. I was one of very few with a half-brother and half-sister, both considerably older than I, so in many ways I was also an only child. My mother was English and worked full-time when most mothers did not. Our family circle of close friends was an odd bunch, a couple with no kids, a gay man, families with troubled kids – several of whom attempted or committed suicide, had addiction problems, and one (a grade school friend) who later killed her father.

My closest childhood friends were also from atypical family circumstances, one was adopted, several were of color. This is not surprising since I was raised by an African American licensed practical nurse who was my nanny, Elizabeth. Henry and Pat left me with her when I was seven weeks old to go to a conference. This pattern continued, and periodically I would stay with Elizabeth in her home where I spent a lot of time exposed to African American culture through activities in her neighborhood and church. Clearly, I was the other in her world and she in mine, but it wasn't until others pointed out the difference that I noticed. I found myself betwixt and between again with one of the most important people in my life. Elizabeth stayed with us in one way or another until I was 18 and she died when I was 21. I'll never forget the sound of her casket closing in her church and the wailing of the women during the service.

For the first 12 years of my life, I spent three weeks every summer in England visiting family where I had no cousins. I was surrounded by Victorian-era grandparents, great aunts and uncles with Victorian views of children and women, and my mother's sister, my aunt, married with no children. My aunt didn't like children, so it was not until I was in my late 20s that I truly developed a relationship with her. The Victorian group wanted me to be English and they were a bit miffed that my mother had married an American. This is ironic because my dad's family is predominantly English and we are related to Lord Burleigh, the adviser to Queen Elizabeth I. Maybe that annoyed them more. Or maybe they were angry that Pat gave up her British citizenship to become a naturalized American citizen. I'll never know. They are all gone now. Have been for years. I am the last of Pat's line. Whichever it was, or something else, I spent my childhood betwixt and between British and American identities.

My place in Henry's extended family was also betwixt and between. I was four years younger than my nearest cousin and four years older than my oldest first cousin once removed. There was no break in the two generations and several of my oldest cousins are old enough to be my parent. There was no room for me to be a kid on either side.

I spent my K–4th grade years at a small, K–8 private school just up the road from my home. It was a small pond and interestingly for the time, my class included several diverse populations and atypical families. I was a relatively happy child and I was friendly with most students in my class. This was the only school experience where I felt I somewhat fit in. My best friend was adopted, and another good friend of mine was the one who later killed her father. She and I had an out-of-school connection. Both our older sisters met and became friends at the same boarding school.

One of my first Punk actions, a stand against authority, happened one Friday at lunch. Students sat at tables headed by teachers and administrators, and on this particular day I was seated at a table headed by the assistant head master. One of the vegetables that day was canned beets. None of us took a beet as they were passed around the table. The assistant head master was furious and said we each had to eat a beet the size of a silver dollar before we all were allowed to leave the table for break. We all sat right through break. He finally had to let us go back to class without eating a beet. We won! Power to the people!

In fourth grade, my best friend decided to go to another girls only prep school for the fifth grade and I followed suit. The population at prep school was less diverse, and most students came from traditional families of local generational privilege with little interest in those outside their own circle. My best friend was still my best friend and I developed some friendships with the other outsiders. By the time I reached seventh grade, the school allowed boys and we had three in our class and I was most friendly with them. In fifth or sixth grade, we read S. E. Hinton's *The Outsiders*, a coming-of-age novel that explored social divisions. It was clear to me that at this school, I was a Greaser, not a Social ("Socs" were wealthy, privileged, upper class, while Greasers represented the working class). I had moved from fitting in to being out. My main activity was horseback riding and during this time I got my own pony, and later a horse. I spent much of my time at the barn and often slept there for the weekends, which kept me from socializing with my school peers. While I connected with the other riders, my deepest connections were with my trainers, my pony, and later, my horse.

My best friend and I decided that ninth grade at prep school would be our last. My best friend moved on to a Friends school. I arrived at my public high school in tenth grade. I was a year ahead of my class in coursework and most of my new peers had been together through elementary school and junior high. Breaking in was difficult. I was still stuck betwixt and between, this time tenth and eleventh grade. Our school allowed smoking, so I was able to hang out with that crowd. Eventually, I aligned with a bunch of misfits that included tenth, eleventh, and twelfth graders. We were a diverse crowd that didn't fit in with the traditional cliques. We had a lot of fun hanging at school, going to house parties, and doing other activities on the weekends. I was still a bit betwixt and between school friends and horse friends. I was still riding and was on to my second horse. This horse and I never connected and that made it easier to walk away. I spent time at the barn and as a riding camp counselor in the summers, but riding ended when I graduated high school. My best friend from high school is still one of my best friends today. We have spent Christmas Eve together at his family home since we were 16. In high school, he hosted an exchange student from England who now lives in London and is another of my closest friends.

My best friend from grade school and I both chose the same college. We were friendly but not close at this stage. Even though she had crossed into my high school social life and dated a guy from my high school, we had been drifting apart. I had a tough time making friends in college and joined a few of the girls who were friendly to me. With them, I became a little sister in a fraternity. I dated a frat brother through most of my sophomore and junior years. Neither of us really fit into the fraternity mold. We mostly just hung out together.

It wasn't until I took a post-graduation trip to Italy that I made two more friends, both men, who are among my closest friends today. After the trip, one joined me in the training program for our first job. The other introduced me to the Philly Punk scene and to my Punk family and Elizabeth Fiend, whom you will meet later in this book.

Like my mother, I am an independent professional woman, divorced many years ago with no children. Most friends I have made as an adult fall into three circles: one group revolved around my job as a fitness professional, another around the Philly Punk scene, and more recently I formed an international group of academic friends from my years of conferencing. Like me, these friends have deviated from normal expectations in some way – married, single, childless by choice, or identify as LGBTQ, or come from a different cultural background. We are all the "other" in some sense. It does seem that I was destined to live life as the other.

1
Debunking academic Punk: How I punked the academy

Subculture as a teaching tool

On a trip to London in the late 1980s, I stumbled on the *Street Style* exhibit curated by Ted Polhemus, a British anthropologist, sociologist, and cultural commentator known for his work on subcultures, fashion, and youth movements, at the Victoria and Albert Museum. The presentation of subcultural styles spoke to me in so many ways personally and piqued my interest into the broader connections between fashion, music, and identity. The catalog for the exhibit became a formative resource for years to come.

At the time I was teaching fashion merchandising in an associate degree program at a proprietary trade school (my first professional teaching gig). History of Costume was one of my courses. The exhibit inspired me to envision a new way to frame the history in a more personal way for the student. I tackled the topic in a reverse engineering kind of way. We examined the current rise of street style to provide an overarching history of fashion. Then we explored subcultural styles and identified the historic references. Next, we traced the references back to their origins. The course ended with the production of a fashion show where students styled and modeled various subcultural styles. The students and I sourced various garments and accessories from family, friends, and thrift shops. Garments and accessories were reworked or made and the looks were styled. I created atmospheric slides and set them to music as a backdrop for the show.

This approach was such a success that I decided to develop another course around the performative aspect of Punk under the guise of visual merchandising. (VM has been my passion because it's all about spectacle.) This time we created the Mad Hatter's Tea Party. (My maker self was a hat designer at the time.) First, we revisited the story and the characters from *Alice in Wonderland*, paying special attention to visual media. Then each student was assigned a character and was charged with making a costume that included a hat. We then constructed an oversized croquet set and acquired picnic tea party accoutrements. On the day of our performance at lunchtime, students dressed at school and we paraded six blocks through the central business district in Philadelphia and set up shop in Rittenhouse Square, a historic and elegant park located in the heart of the district. This park is a high-traffic space and frequented by people eating lunch outside. It was a beautiful day and the park provided a huge audience. We staked out our space and immediately started a game of croquet. The crowd reaction ran the gamut from amazed and intrigued to gobsmacked and incredulous. After a few rounds of croquet, we sat on blankets and enjoyed our picnic tea party, cleaned up, and returned to the school.

These experiences formed the framework for my teaching methodology for the rest of my career. Punk allowed me to be a dynamic performative lecturer. My DIY (do it yourself) skills and attitude that "I can do anything" granted me the opportunity to empower my students, building their confidence and instilling joy in learning.

The *Street Style* exhibit cycled back into my psyche several years later at Drexel University. We were expanding our courses based on visual merchandising, notably a course that focused on Exhibit Design. The course was designed for seniors, providing them with an opportunity to synthesize the business, research, and design skills they had learned throughout their course of study. Each student did a deep dive into a youth subculture and created a display that included a two-dimensional art work, three-dimensional build, and a digital experience that reflected the subculture. For several years, the individual displays were combined into a group gallery exhibition titled *Style Tribes*, first mounted in Old City and later West Philadelphia. Students were responsible for their producing individual displays, creating the group display, marketing, and planning the opening event. The class ran its course, but I was far from done with the topic.

Punk at the PCA

In 2005, my colleague introduced me to the Popular Culture Association (PCA). As a teaching professor, I had not been involved in academic research, but the PCA intrigued me. As

I was a program director with a research professor on my team, I wanted to understand the academic side so I could support him in his professional journey. I debuted at the PCA with a presentation about Gothic Lolitas (a common character pairing from cosplay, which is the act of dressing as a character generally from fictional work that originated in Japan), and subsequently took a tour through Skull & Crossbones; I explored the symbol and its use from the golden age of piracy to modern subcultures and cultivated a perennial "fashion pack" of global scholars.

One of the early presentations I attended was focused specifically on fashion, music, and identity, and this scholar's work provided much of the framework, objectives, and methodologies for my project. My participation in the PCA culminated in the founding of the Punk Culture Area and I was the inaugural area chair. Timing really is everything. The area was born just as Punk was gaining huge academic interest as a group of Punk-era youth who had become scholars were participating the conference scene.

The PCA accepted a variety of presentation formats, allowing our area to accept all sorts of submissions from strict academic papers to performances. Each year we included at least one roundtable discussion and a meetup where we created a conference Zine. One year we had a performance with a Gatling gun and a graffiti wall. My participation both broadened and deepened my understanding of my own experience and research and opened me up to a larger global perspective of Punk Culture.

To me, the most interesting presentation over all those years was a paper submitted by a young Irish woman scholar. It was based on anecdotal interviews about how both Catholic and Protestant Irish youth in Northern Ireland in the late 1970s/early 1980s came together in a space that hosted Punk bands. I don't remember the name of the bar, but a quick bit of research with the help of ChatGPT lead me to these comments that very closely match her father's anecdotes that she shared in the presentation.

"The [Harp] bar was situated in what was a rundown corner of a Belfast city center that was deserted at night due to the troubles. It became a relatively safe venue for both Protestant and Catholic Punks to mix and listen to the large number of local bands that were forming, inspired by Punk". "At a time when the religious divide in Northern Ireland was most pronounced, we had kids from both sides of the community coming together in the name of music" (Hooley and Sullivan, 2010, p. 83). "It really was the first time I can remember that significant numbers of young people from all sections and classes of community, and from both sides of the sectarian divide were able to meet up and get to know each other, initially drawn together by their enthusiasm for this new music and lifestyle" (Hooley and Sullivan, 2010, pp. 141–142).

As noted earlier, Bloody Sunday in Ireland had a profound effect on me and created a familial rift with my conservative English grandmother. I have followed the tension known as "The Troubles" throughout my life. The conflict officially ended with the Good Friday Agreement of 1998, supposedly. It was amazing to me that Punk could bridge that chasm, even more so because I had visited Belfast for a conference in July of 2009 and was quite aware of the circumstances at that time. I had taken a Black Taxi tour through areas of the "Troubles," and there was no way the divide was over. What I saw were blocks of streets with corrugated metal walls topped with razor wire and a few doors down the center. I asked our driver/tour guide when they would come down. His reply was, "Oh, maybe in 25 years." I am sorry the young scholar did not continue with the study.

My standing at the PCA positioned me as a credible source on all things Punk. Yep – little old teaching professor me done good in the academic arena.

Debunking academic Punk studies pre-2000

It didn't take long for academics to begin researching Punk as a youth subculture. What exists in the canon includes work by such scholars as: Hebdige, Le Blanc, Evans and Norton, Frith, and Douglas. These authors examined youth subculture through a variety of lenses from 1966 to 1999. Each has characterized Punk in a variety of ways, but the academic blinders have pigeonholed and marginalized the movement. Much of the support is based in old research – even that predating the Punk era.

In the late 1970s, Hebdige, a British cultural theorist, sociologist, and author of the seminal book *Subculture: The Meaning of Style*, classified Punk as working class, British, and male. This totally negates Punk in the United States, Australia, and worldwide, and ignores the many women who participated in the scene all over the world. In 1999, Lauraine LeBlanc, sociologist and author of *Pretty in Punk: Girl's Gender Resistance in a Boy's Subculture*, added her voice and tried to address the female; however, she describes a scene of marginalized women participating in a movement based on resistance and style. To her credit, she proffered a more inclusive view of the scene, discussing the variety of players as noted in I Am PUNK.

More recent research has been presented from 2001 on, however, much of the published work focuses on Punk as an influence on recent subcultures. This presented a conundrum in providing current, relevant, and credible sources valued by the academy. There has been and continues to be, a robust library of Punk-focused books published for the mass market.

Two mass market books released during my years of research, seemed far more relevant to the Punk scene. Seth Godin's *Tribes: We Need You to Lead Us* and Ralph Heath's *Celebrating Failure: The Power of Taking Risks, Making Mistakes, and Thinking Big* not only explore two central themes important to Punk, but they also take a Punk approach to writing and presentation. Short chapters, like the infamous two-minute Punk song, barrage the reader with a single concept, short and sweet. Each text contributed to the further framing of my work.

In *Tribes: We Need You to Lead Us*, Godin states, the only thing that holds people back from creating change is lack of Faith – that you can do it, it is worth doing and that failure won't destroy you (Godin, 2008, p. 71). When we meet Elizabeth Fiend, we will see that curiosity became her driving force. Change is interesting and she can't wait to see what happens next (Godin, 2008, pp. 63–64). Engaged, passionate, committed to challenging the status quo, Elizabeth becomes a heretic for social change by Godin's definition (Godin, 2008, p. 49).

Heath believes in the greatness of failure and opens *Celebrating Failure: The Power of Taking Risks, Making Mistakes, and Thinking Big* with the following statement, "Failure and defeat are life's greatest teachers." He goes on to explain that for this to be true, mistakes must be forgiven. Only then can one embrace risk-taking, possible failure, and subsequent success. Sounds like the Ramones (an early Punk band from New York known for fast-paced, three-chord songs, leather jackets, and shaggy hair), right?

An ethnographic study, responses to a central survey, one-on-one interviews, autobiographical anecdotes, and analysis round out my research with location and time-based accounts. These are the gems that support my thesis about the scene in Philadelphia.

2
What Punk is: What Punk is not

I have found that when I say the word "Punk" to the public, a vision generally pops into their head. It is that of a male with a mohawk in a studded and painted motorcycle jacket with a ripped tee, jeans, and Doc Martens. Think Sid Vicious, the bassist for the Sex Pistols and you've got it. This is a London look from the 1970s and you can still find it worldwide today.

The Great Rock 'n' Roll Swindle – NOT the mockumentary

It's important to note that this styling originated with London fashion designer and entrepreneur Vivienne Westwood, and former New York Dolls (an American glam rock band often credited as the precursor to Punk) manager Malcolm Maclaren as they worked together to create the band the Sex Pistols. The Pistols are often described as the least punk, Punk band ever because they were built around a contrived ideology and aesthetic.

McLaren, and to some degree Westwood, were interested in the situationist movement, a philosophy that came about in the late 1950s. The proponents included revolutionary avant-garde artists, intellectuals, and political theorists who criticized the commercialization of daily existence and the widespread impact of mass media. Central to this point of view is the concept of spectacle that highlights how everyday life is dominated by the passive consumption of commodities and media, leading to a society where appearances and superficiality overshadow genuine human connections and experiences. This spectacle perpetuates a system where individuals are disconnected from their own lives and the real world, reinforcing capitalist structures and alienation. Sound familiar?

British filmmaker, DJ, and musician Don Letts, known for his influential role in the Punk and reggae London scenes of the 1970s and 1980s, commented on the Sex Pistols in *Punk Style, Articles of Interest #6* in 2018. He recounted that the Sex Pistols were built to shock in the same vein as a situationist spectacle. He further affirms Punk music came from the United States, but soundly declares that the British gave Punk style (Letts, 2018). Nevertheless, the Pistols became an international sensation and got a lot of press in a time when everyone consumed the same media, so their image became THE Punk image for the general population. But this is a very narrow view of Punk.

The Sex Pistols officially broke up in 1978, leaving more room for other Punk bands to perform their strain of Punk music. By the 1980s, the Punk genre had grown to include many more influences, such as ska, electronica, spoken word, and so on. Scenes were hyperlocal. They continued to celebrate rebellion, DIY, and antiestablishment ideologies, but music, fashion, and personal style were distinctive to place. A breakthrough by Nirvana on MTV in 1991 resulted in industry investment in the second Punk music wave in the 1990s including the band Green Day. Billie Joe

Armstrong said it himself: "Punk is not just the sound [...] punk is a lifestyle."

What Punk is not

It is also important to note that Punk Culture is NOT solely Punk Music. Often, the term "Punk" is conflated with Punk Music and when this happens, the argument of authenticity always ensues. Every year at the PCA, there was some ridiculous squabble over whether this band, place, fashion, and so on was Punk or not and who was more authentic. It was so tedious.

My go-to guy on Punk Music is Brian Cogan, professor, scholar, and author of *The Encyclopedia of Punk*. Incidentally, I met Brian through the PCA, but we have a Philly connection. His wife is from Philly and played in a Philly band. I was acquainted with his wife and the band back in the day. Brian's book is about Punk Music, but he clearly states his point of view, preempting the authenticity argument. Brian says, 'Punk rock is not so much about "What happened and when?" as it is about "What's been going on, and where is it happening now?"' (Cogan, 2008, p. viii).

Brian goes further during an interview posted July 31, 2012, titled "Out of His Mind: Brian Cogan and the Writing of the Encyclopedia of Punk," for RiffRaf, a Brooklyn blog that focuses on alternative, indie, rock, Punk, pop, R & B, and folk, when answering this question: Why do you think you're drawn to the Punk ethos?

> The punk ethos is about developing a set of critical tools to look at the world. It's not to divorce yourself from the world. To ask, "How do you affect the people in your environment?" Punk was never meant to be exclusionary.

> When you say, "This is what it has to be" is when you lose the spirit.
>
> John Holmstrom and Legs McNeil from *Punk Magazine* said that punk ended around '79, '80 or '81. I think it never ended. I think it pre-dated CBGB's. I think it's still going on. Punk is a cultural virus that pops up independently of where it should have been stamped out. (Cogan, 2012)

US rock journalist and former editor of *CREEM* magazine, Dave Marsh, coined the term "Punk" in 1971 to describe 1960s garage rock. If you want a solid definition of Punk Music, *Wikipedia* provides one, as summarized here:

Rooted in garage rock and reacting to excessive 1970s rock ballads, Punk rock developed in the United States, the United Kingdom, and Australia. Bands created fast, raw, and short music, often featuring political, antiestablishment lyrics, and practiced a DIY ethic, with many bands self-producing their albums, distributing them through informal channels and using guerilla marketing.

So, what then is Punk?

The commonly accepted Punk origin story is that it began in the United States (Detroit and New York) and the United Kingdom (London). This origin story sometimes includes Australia, likely because it was, and still is, tightly connected in many ways with the UK. In a Red Hand Files post, Issue #268, published in January 2024, Australian musician Nick Cave, front man of the Birthday Party and of Nick Cave and the Bad Seeds, wrote, "I still argue that The Saints [a Punk band from Brisbane, Australia, credited with one of the earliest punk records, a debut single titled "I'm Stranded"] started punk rock" (Cave, 2024).

In the UK, the movement was connected to disaffected working-class youth who had few opportunities in the economy of the time. In the United States, it was a rebellion against the peace and love hippie movement. In both countries, the United Kingdom and the United States, Punks took a more aggressive performative approach expressing frustration and anger with political systems, oppression, and social injustice.

On a trip to Sydney, Australia, for a conference in 2011, I was fortunate to see *The 80s Are Back*, an exhibit recounting the era through the lens of ordinary Australians (Allon). The artifacts and materials shown related to Australian Punk, confirm a decidedly London Punk look.

As Colegrave and Sullivan state in their book *Punk the Definitive Record of a Revolution*, Punk is a collective group of free spirits who were united by questioning authority for oneself as an individual. Their spirit and attitude were based in subversion and that resulted in their being seen as the "other" (Colegrave and Sullivan, 2005, pp. 12, 13).

Punk is a movement that rejects mainstream culture and focuses on moving toward the new while reacting to the societal norms and belief systems of the time. Punk action is based on response and revolution, creating empowerment, agency, and voice to gain social and political capital. The movement grows like a virus. Commercial success is not the end goal.

Once something is commodified, it is no longer Punk. Punk must constantly transform its cultural production to remain Punk. The need to transform is built into the system and that allows the movement to mutate and grow. There is never a shortage of disaffected youth, so the movement continues to pop up globally, often dovetailing with political swings too far toward authoritarianism.

Artists on the scene are creative cultural producers of fashion, music, and media that are specific to the subculture and position the subculture as the "other." These cultural products include signs and symbols, easily recognized by the tribe. As like-minded thinkers, Punks create communities and build infrastructures. Using DIY, Punks construct physical spaces, build an audience, and form their own institutions.

Over 50 years, these cultural spaces and institutions have provided the infrastructure and framework to support Punk culture and lifestyle.

Bringing it all together – my definition of Punk

First and foremost, Punk is one of the last two analog subcultures, with hip-hop being the other. While both subcultures exist in today's digital world, it is important to remember that when both began and spread, communication was non-digital, records were vinyl, media was comparatively small. I grew up with a black and white television, three major networks, three UHF channels, and one public broadcasting station. The world was more local. Global information, aside from what counted as news, was slow to arrive. Fashion is a good example. High-end designers set the trends in Europe and you wouldn't see much about them until about three months later when the fashion magazines covering the shows hit the newsstands. Today you can watch Fashion Week shows live or immediately after on your phone!

Recently, Survey Respondent 9, who grew up in the mountains about a two-and-a-half-hour drive from Philadelphia, shared her television experience with me. She lived in the Poconos, a popular area for both winter and summer activities. Born out of a quest for better television reception in rural areas, her hometown had some form of cable television access since the late 1940s!

This CATV system allowed her access to a variety of television channels from Pennsylvania, New Jersey, and New York. This facilitated her exposure to a broad variety of alternative culture, most notably *Night Flight*, a late-night cult series that originally aired from 1981 to 1989. It was one of the first outlets for Americans to see music documentaries, and music videos presented as a serious art form. According to *Wikipedia*, *Night Flight* included episodes of New Wave Theater, hosted by Harvard-educated musician Peter Ivers, and created and produced by David Jove (a Canadian director, producer, and writer of underground and alternative music films), and *Billboard* magazine editor Ed Ochs. Episodes showcased Punk and New Wave bands such as Fear, Bad Religion, the Dead Kennedys, and the Circle Jerks. The show ended in 1983 when Ivers was found bludgeoned to death in his apartment.

Cable networks started to grow in the early 1980s. In 1981, MTV hit the scene with 24-hour music videos and the march toward

"Video Killed the Radio Star" began in earnest. This gave bands access to a wider national and global audience, but as technology giveth, so does it taketh away. Pre-video, individuals each had their own memories, visuals, and connections to songs. I can still remember every word my grade school best friend and I sang to Barry Manilow's 1978 "Copacabana." Our story revolved around a summer experience we shared in Atlantic City before we went to separate high schools. Once a video is seen, it can't be unseen, and the result is that everyone who sees a video has the same visual. It's the same with books made into movies.

The premise of the present book is based on my personal Punk experience grounded in my thesis, that Punk includes the following:

- Three key features: bricolage, DIY, and transformation;
- One traditional value: family; and
- A heavy dose of satire, sarcasm, and parody as the most common forms of personal expression.

Combine these with the tenets of Punk:

1. Punk artists are creative and cultural producers.
2. Punks reject mainstream culture, move toward the new, and react to the conventions of the time (response/revolution/activism).
3. Punks are like-minded thinkers who create community and build infrastructures.
4. Through DIY, Punks create spaces, build an audience, and form their own institutions.
5. Cultural products – fashion, music, media are specific to the subculture and position the subculture as the other.

3
It's a Philly thing: Badass things happen in Philly

> *"[Punk] was shows in basements, or small bars, or churches, generally small places, put on by my peers. It was personal, not stadium rock."* – Survey Respondent 11, questionnaire response, 2007

Philadelphia's geographic location positioned the city as a crossroads between New York City and Washington, DC. See? Even today I live betwixt and between. The local scene included talent from what is known as the tristate area, Philadelphia proper and surrounding Pennsylvania counties, Delaware, Montgomery, Bucks, the Lehigh Valley, South Jersey, and Delaware. Savvy Philadelphia booking agents often booked more well-known bands for a show in Philly as a stop between NYC and DC.

Punks build their own infrastructure, create DIY spaces, build an audience, and form their own institutions. The movement grows like a virus – grassroots. Commercial success is not the end goal.

One of the most notable of these Philly spaces was Jeff Jenkins' basement in West Philadelphia. Known as the West Side Club,

Jeff hosted many touring bands in addition to local talent. The West Side Club is a prime example of a Philly Punk institution. Just this year, 2024, I attended an Ultra Bomb show at a local music venue, Theater for the Living Arts, aka TLA, featuring Greg Norton from Hüsker Dü on bass. Early in the set, he looked out at the audience and asked, "Hey, how many of you saw me in Jeff Jenkins' basement?" There were a fair number of hands up including mine.

Punk is performative and basement shows were in intimate, small spaces where the audience and band became one, performing together to create the spectacle. I attended a bunch of shows in basements, but I think I was in the West Side Club where I learned why mobsters and interrogators beat people with a rubber hose. It was a Halloween show and I went as the Greek goddess Medusa, the one with snakes for hair. It was easy. I wired a few rubber snakes into my hair and I carried a slightly larger one as a staff. As part of my personal performance, I periodically smacked my friend with the rubber snake as we danced in the pit. It didn't seem to be a problem at the time, but the next day, he had deep tissue bruising where I'd hit him. Who knew? Because of the flexibility, a rubber hose can inflict soft tissue injury without leaving external marks. In fact, a beating with a rubber hose is considered inhumane and a violation of human rights. Fortunately, my snake was not as dense as a rubber hose and I didn't hit him in any organs, so the bruising did not lead to permanent damage to my friend.

As one of the renowned DJs from 91.7, WKDU, Drexel University's student-run radio station, Jeff Jenkins, along with Eddie "Hacksaw" from 88.5, WXPN, the University of

Pennsylvania's radio station, exposed the region to alternative music. These men were pivotal in the promotion and the shaping of the underground Philly music scene. These two stations were also integral in spreading the word about local shows. Remember, this was the analog era, so there was no social media. WKDU broadcast *Philly Happenings*, which featured local and regional shows. The list was long. You had to commit to listening to the entire segment, just like I waited to hear school closing numbers when I was a kid. If you didn't, you were sure to miss something great, whether it was a snow day or a great show. It required laser focus to get all the info. I was lucky that many of my group were WKDU DJs and program directors, both male and female, who had direct access to the copy and connections to the promoters and the bands. Still today, WXPN is the keeper of the WXPN concert calendar, the online go-to if you are looking for all the shows in Philly and beyond.

My Philly scene experience was unique. My circle of friends were primarily interested in the music and many would be classified as LeBlanc's old-school Punks. Much like the Punk movement, our group grew like a virus that diffused from a central group of people involved with WKDU in the early 1980s. Women were important players in our tribe and fully participated in the scene as content creators, musicians, managers, shows, the pit. Two major bars hosting Punk bands on the scene, JC Dobbs and Doc Watson's, had female booking agents who were well respected on the national scene. Much of the larger scene reflected Philly, a diverse city where everyone knew everyone. For the most part, subcultures got along and serious drugs weren't rampant.

So many spaces and places

I've told you about Jeff Jenkins' basement already. This was just one of many of the Punk spaces in Philadelphia. It was a different town then, betwixt and between the decline of manufacturing and the rise of the service economy. This shift created unemployment and urban decay in some neighborhoods and revitalization in others. Culture, history, and architectural heritage attracted visitors, but there were significant crime and safety issues, and progress was SLOW! In many ways the Punk scene benefited from both sides of the coin. There were plenty of bars looking for music and there were plenty of abandoned spaces looking to be used.

There are way too many spaces to mention and I would never be able to list them all. Some had long lives and still exist. Others were temporary or transient (pop-ups before they were a thing). Groups of Punks tended to cluster together in several key parts of the city, primarily West Philadelphia, Center City, Old City, and South Street in the 1980s. As sections gentrified, the scene spread to Northern Liberties and Kensington, although there was a venue, the Starlite Ballroom, right near the Frankford El (short for elevated) stop in the 1980s when Kensington was on the fringe. Like all neighborhoods in Philadelphia, each area had its own flavor. Often the hyperlocal scenes would revolve around one or two shared houses, and depending on the density of the area, there were few or many clubs for all ages and those over the legal drinking age. There were even a few far-flung spaces, notably City Gardens in Trenton, New Jersey, and Club Pizzaz in Northeast Philly.

As usual, I had met up with my hyperlocal group one evening and we headed out for a show. I had no idea where we were going or who we were going to see. We headed to the subway and took the El to the northeast and worked our way over to Club Pizzazz, an all-ages venue. I don't remember who the headliner was, but one of the opening acts was No Means No (a Canadian Punk band from Victoria, British Columbia). It was the first time I heard one of my favorite songs, "Dad" and the first time I set eyes on my ex-husband. Boy, was he hot! He was at the show with a Punk crowd that revolved around the band Flag of Democracy. (F.O.D., as they are known, is a hardcore band formed in 1982 in Ambler, a suburb of Philadelphia.) He made it his business to be where I was for the next few weeks. We started dating, lived together, later married, and eventually divorced. His mom told me that he had come home from the first night we met and told her, "I met the girl I'm going to marry tonight."

Wild West Philly – more than a More Fiends song

The Schuylkill River, a Dutch name meaning "hidden river," was originally called Ganoshowanna by the Lenape tribes in this area. It is one of two rivers that define the boundaries of east and west Philadelphia. The other is the Delaware River that marks the easternmost boundary of the city, defining the boundary between Pennsylvania and New Jersey. In the eighteenth and nineteenth centuries, West Philadelphia, was comprised of rural estates, farm lands, and two important and still thriving educational institutions, the University of Pennsylvania, founded in 1740, and Drexel University, founded as the Drexel Institute of Technology in 1891.

There was more physical space in West Philly. The historic homes were much larger and grander than those in many other sections of Philadelphia and many still exist to this day. With the development of public transportation, the city grew and this area became a lively residential and commercial hub. In the twentieth century, West Philly developed into a diverse community with a dynamic cultural scene contributing to the arts, education, and civil rights. Today, many of the neighborhoods surrounding both universities have gentrified. One neighborhood, Mantua, bordering the west of Drexel's modern sprawl, continues to struggle. Built in 1895 for families of modest means, homes and streets in Mantua were dense with small, two-story row homes with no gardens. In the mid-1900s, it became home to many of the factory workers in various industries in Philadelphia. As factories closed in the 1970s and 1980s, this area lost over 30 percent of the population. Those who remained were mostly unemployed. This area remains one of the poorest neighborhoods in the city today. In 2003, Drexel University established the Lindy Center for Civic Engagement, which supports the community through student and faculty involvement in various projects and works closely with community partners to affect positive change in this area. It was named one of President Barack Obama's Promise Zones in 2014.

My favorite group house in West Philadelphia was the Fat House, a large home shared by three very large men who hosted many parties on the corner of 47th Street and Chester Avenue. I still pass this house on occasion. Other spaces included Clark Park and Abe's Steaks. Clark Park held festivals that featured music from local Punk bands. More Fiends (Elizabeth and Allen Fiend's

Philly-based anarchist Punk band who were masters at mash-ups before they became a thing), who were part of the West Philly crew, played there.

Abe's Steaks (a Philly cheesesteak shop at 20 South 40th Street) was an institution, hosting shows in a small room in the back of the steak shop. Elizabeth Fiend has by far the best story about Abe's Steaks and it predates my meeting her. (You'll meet her soon, I promise.) She recounted it to me in a recent conversation. During a show at Abe's, More Fiends did a jam themed "What's in the Bag?" while the crowd passed a large bag around. The bag was essentially stage diving in reverse, toward the stage. Finally, the bag made it to the stage and to the band member it belonged to. He opened the bag to reveal … his new prosthetic leg and proceeded to put it on. Talk about performance! One of the band members from another local band, the Dead Milkmen (a Philadelphia Punk band known for irreverent humor, satirical lyrics, quirkiness, a DIY ethos, and memorable live performances), told Elizabeth it was the greatest story of his life.

Three cabaret music venues were owned by Alan Berger and his partner and entertainment manager, Steve Mountain of Cornerstone Management, from 1980–1994. One, 23 East, was in Ardmore, close to where I grew up in Lower Merion. The Ambler Cabaret 57 East Butler Avenue was of course in Ambler, Pennsylvania. (You might remember that the Ambler area was home to the Philly band F.O.D.) The Chestnut Cabaret, by far the largest of the three, was at 38th and Chestnut Streets in West Philadelphia. The trio of spaces hosted over 500 national acts a year representing a variety of music styles, including The Pretenders and The Ramones, as well as local talent featuring

Robert Hazard, The Hooters, as well as local favorites Beru Review and Tommy Conwell (who was a friend of mine from high school), and the Young Rumblers. There's an impressive list on the Chestnut Cabaret *Wikipedia* page.

I saw many bands at the Chestnut, but the one that stands out to me the most is a Serial Killers (a local Philly Punk band known as "the only band that splatters" Punk, meets slasher flick, meets pro wrestling) show. My favorite Serial Killers album is *Roadside Rendezvous* and my favorite track is "Dead Bitch." The standout lyric: "Dead Bitch lying in a ditch." A search on the Internet pulls up a pdf shared by Michael Erlewine that includes a show on November 28, 1988, that looks likely with Serial Killers / Deadspot / More Fiends / Orifice. Why does this show stand out? Well, I was standing well back from the pit, but a young London-style Punk came elbowing his way through and inadvertently caught me in the ribs. That's when I learned how painful bruised ribs are. My side gig was aerobics instructor. Teaching with a bruised rib was no joke. I felt the pain with every breath for a couple of weeks. Guess that was fate's way of paying me back for the rubber snake incident.

Philly CBD – that's central business district, not cannabidiol

The Center City entertainment scene was home to lots of bars and clubs, most notably The East Side Club, located at 1229 Chestnut from 1981–1984, and The Kennel Club, at 12th and Walnut. Both were members-only establishments. Doc Watson's was a stone's throw away at 216 South 11th Street, next to the campus of Jefferson University/Hospital. Affectionately known as Doc's, the bar offered three floors of entertainment behind a facade of a traditional English pub. That's what you got on the first floor. Head up to the second, and you got a pub and live music venue. Still not your jam? Head up to the third floor for a dance party. Prices were low, there was never a cover, and entertainment appealed to a broad range of tastes. They catered to their community and were a beloved local. It's now a bar called Strangelove's that has a decent happy hour.

The Trocadero, known locally as "The Troc," is located at 10th and Arch Streets in Philadelphia's Chinatown. It opened in 1870 as a vaudeville theater. Over the years, it expanded its programming to include opera, burlesque, and live music. It's a treasured cultural landmark that drew eclectic and diverse audiences until its closure in 2019. According to a *Philly Voice* article dated November 1, 2022, The Troc secured $2.5 million in funding for a complete renovation to transform it into a concert and entertainment space with a full-service restaurant (*Philly Voice*, 2022). With the Troc located near the Philadelphia convention center, this plan will likely be a great success.

We went to the Troc for all sorts of programming including live shows and film screenings. My graduate school artwork was exhibited as part of a live event. My favorite memory of the Troc was when KeN (who you will hear more about later) opened for the Psychedelic Furs (aka Psych Furs), a British new wave band known best for the song "Pretty in Pink" that was used by John Hughes for his 1986 film of the same name. One of the women from our extended group married Fur bassist Tim Butler in Disneyland and several of our group attended. That connection got KeN the opening gig. It was truly a fun night.

Historic Philly – independents ignited

Old City is the historic section of Philadelphia dating back to William Penn, the city's founding father. This area is home to Independence Hall, where our forefathers signed the Declaration of Independence. As the city grew so did the manufacturing sector. In the late nineteenth and the early twentieth century, Philadelphia became known as the "Workshop of the World," making it a center of innovation and craftsmanship that continues today. Old City became an industrial area, but as textile and garment manufacturing moved offshore in the late 1970s and early 1980s, these large, abandoned buildings needed repurposing and revitalization. Driven by the restoration of historic buildings and the conversion of industrial spaces into trendy, modern loft apartments, Old City attracted artists and young professionals to the area. They in turn drove the development of trendy boutiques, galleries, eateries, and nightlife. But not everything was bright and shiny. Philly always has some grit. Khyber Pass was a favorite dive bar, music venue. It's now a gastropub serving regional Southern favorites. (The building has been a bar since the 1850s and was a speakeasy during Prohibition.) Upstairs at Nicks (closed in 1999) over Nick's Roast Beef was another dive bar with music, both were dingy. You never wanted to touch the bar top in either place. They were sticky and edgy venues that hosted bands in small spaces. Setlist.fm chronicles many national and local bands played them both.

South Street – where do all the hippies meet?

South Street, South Street. Put it together and you have a lyric from the popular 1963 song titled "South Street" by the Orlons (a Philadelphia R & B group popular in the 1960s), and it put South Street in Philadelphia on the national radar. In the early days of Philadelphia, South Street marked the southern boundary of William Penn's city. Since the 1960s and 1970s, it has been a gathering place for various counterculture movements with an eclectic mix of shops, restaurants, and music venues. When we talk about South Street in Philadelphia, we are talking about the east side of Broad Street, the north/south central street that marks the middle of Center City proper.

Like the Trocadero, the Theater of the Living Arts (TLA) is a historical venue that anchored South Street. A 700-seat nickelodeon, the "Crystal Palace," opened in 1908. Following the trajectory of live entertainment, it transitioned into a concert hall in 1927, followed by the "New Palace Theatre," a Warner Bros. cinema in 1941. Transitions continued from a live theater and beatnik house in the 1960s to an art house movie theater in the 1970s where the cult classic *The Rocky Horror Picture Show* (described by *Wikipedia* as "a 1975 independent musical comedy horror film") became a huge success. There were weekly showings with audience participation, audience members dressing as their favorite characters, acting out scenes, singing along, and enjoying Pop Rocks, a candy that exploded in your mouth. It was certainly akin to a performative Punk rock spectacle. I wasn't a regular, but I attended on several occasions. TLA finally became a music venue in 1988. Acquired by Live Nation Entertainment in 2006, the space continues to thrive.

Just a few doors east, at 3rd and South Streets, is JC Dobbs, a local dive bar that became an iconic Philadelphia music venue, hosting many national bands including Green Day and Nirvana before they gained national fame. One of my fondest memories of Dobbs was a show in the late 1980s. It was a great local bill, Trained Attack Dogs (a short-lived three-to-five-piece West Philly band that debuted in 1986 on WKDU), The She Males (a metal/Punk, performative band with a name based on a porn tape titled "She Male Encounters"), and Dead Spot (a crossover metal/Punk/hardcore band). This lineup suited both me and my ex, who loved She Males and Dead Spot. Trained Attack Dogs was more my thing and one of my favorite local bands, 100 percent Philly. TAD played in many local spaces, but most often Revival and released albums on the local label Rave Records.

Located on 5th and Gaskill Streets was my local Punk group home. This tiny house became our meeting space. It was too small for epic parties (although that didn't keep us from trying), but it was within walking distance to Old City, Center City, and South Street venues. Other celebrated spaces on South Street moving west included Grendel's Lair, a 500-seat cabaret theater at 5th and South, The Ripley Music Hall, formerly the Hippodrome at 610 South Street, and Bacchanal at 13th and South that showcased artists, playwrights, and music.

Abandoned spaces = pop-up performance

On the east side of South street, the venue parade ended with the Love Club, aka Love Hall, located on Broad (14th Street) and South Streets on the edge of the University of the Arts (formerly Philadelphia College of Arts and recently infamously closed in seven days!) campus. The Love Club attracted musicians, poets, performance artists, and visual artists, and became a breeding ground for various types of underground activity. The building was severely damaged by a fire in 1983 and was condemned and torn down in 1985 or 1986. No building, no problem. The Philly industrial band Sink Manhattan (described as truly a bang-on-the-metal industrial band with a set that looked like a junkyard on the Freedom Has No Bounds website) co-opted the space and put on a show. Many of the women in our circle thought these guys were hotties!

Record stores

Record stores are magical places of discovery and of sharing music and scene information, central to the making and sustaining of a scene. Acting as cultural hubs, they not only foster a sense of community, but also provide a conduit for local and independent artists to reach new audiences and fans through in-store performances and events. Like museums, libraries, or historic institutions, they preserve, archive, and catalog physical artifacts linked to the history of the scene.

Philadelphia Memories Blog describes 3rd Street Jazz & Rock as the granddaddy of local record stores in a September 21, 2019, post titled "Neighborhood Record Stores." Gone, but not forgotten was the legendary 3rd Street Jazz & Rock record store, which had a decent run from 1972 to 1998 on N. 3rd Street, Old City. With an informed staff, it was an alternative music mecca, especially for imports, bootlegs, and hard-to-find artists. Appropriately, the rock genre was in the basement. It was a lo-fi shopping experience, sorting through records identified with handmade sign labels. It was like a treasure hunt, filled with discovery as you searched for your pot of gold.

Dan DaLuca of the *Philadelphia Inquirer* reports, the Philadelphia Record Exchange located at 5th and South Streets from 1985 to 2012, was founded by co-owners Jacy Webster and Greg Harris (currently the CEO of the Rock & Roll Hall of Fame in Cleveland). They had been selling their personal collections of rock, jazz, and blues at the legendary secondhand book store, The Book Trader, formerly located at 4th and South Streets (now located on N. 2nd Street in Old City). Since 2012, the Philadelphia Record Exchange has been in Fishtown (home to DiPinto Guitars and many music venues, from intimate bars to larger performance spaces). Between the venues and the musicians who live in neighborhood, Fishtown is alive with music, a perfect mix for one of the notable and sustaining record stores in Philadelphia.

According to the Downtown West Chester Directory, Creep Records began in 1993 as a record label out of West Chester, Pennsylvania, about 30 miles southwest of the city. With three locations in Northern Liberties, Port Richmond, and West Chester, Pennsylvania, going strong for more than a decade, Creep Record stores are a hub for old and new. I just saw that my new favorite Punk band, Spiritual Cramp (formed in San Francisco in

2017), played an in-store show on June 20, 2024. A friend and I caught their show that same night at a current popular venue, Underground Arts.

It may be instructive to tell you how I learned about the band. I was with three friends in Swarthmore, about 20 miles southwest of the city, during the holiday season in 2023. We were doing some local shopping and were directed to a space, not a record store per se, that had a collection of interesting artifacts and collectibles, many surrounding music, film, and video. There was a selection of vintage vinyl. As we were chatting with the owner, he mentioned the record that was playing was this new-to-him band, Spiritual Cramp, and they would be playing the First Unitarian Church on Valentine's Day, 2024. (Yes, church. We have several church venues that host Punk shows in Philly.) Three of us got tickets and went. Two of us liked them enough to go back last week (June 20, 2024). They have really grown in stage presence and performance from February to June. We are hooked.

Today, Philadelphia's Punk music labels have persisted, adapting to new technologies and market trends. Record stores continue to champion local Punk talent, releasing albums, organizing shows, and preserving the DIY ethos that defines Philadelphia's Punk music scene.

Philly Punk style

> "When I was younger and had a more 'anti-establishment' look, I definitely identified with a certain type of person because of it. it said to me that we were brave, that we refused to accept the status quo of the Reagan era and its warmongering, consumerism, wastefulness,

closed-mindedness, conservatism, etc." –Respondent 7, response to questionnaire, 2007

If anyone told me in graduate school that I would include a reference to Roland Barthes' book *The Fashion System* in a book written by me, I would have said they were joking, but here we are. I could not stand this book. It was my cure for insomnia. I'd pick it up to read, and minutes later my eyes would close and I'd drop off into a deep sleep. The ideas in this book weren't the issue. It was the convoluted way they were presented. Likely this was because the original book was published in French in 1967. My copy was an English translation published in 1983.

In essence, Barthes' theory endeavors to understand the meaning of clothing. Barthes applies semiotics, the study of signs and symbols and their use or interpretation, to fashion, specifically fashion magazines. Signs and sign systems in fashion are ideas and ideologies translated through clothing. It's a useful framework to analyze and understand subcultural style.

Local Punk style

Philly Punk style generally falls into one basic look that includes several foundational pieces, personalized with a lot of variation, particularly for women.

Unisex Look: This look was worn by most men and some women. It consisted of a leather jacket, jeans, a band T-shirt and/or flannel shirt, and army boots. Jacket variations included leather biker jackets (often painted and studded), leather moto jackets, leather or military long coats, denim jackets, and denim vests. Variations on footwear included biker boots, or Doc Martens. Slogan T-shirts were a variation for band T-shirts.

Women's Looks: Philly Punk women modified the basic look with these further variations: leopard coats, men's suit jackets, and denim jackets; miniskirts and leggings, fishnets, or tights; a vintage dress or slip. And *"Boots. Always Boots!"* – Respondent 11, questionnaire response, 2007

Looks were further personalized with alterations and decoration of clothing and various adornments – hardware, jewelry, various haircuts and hair colors, and tattoos.

In Barthes' semiotics, anything in culture can be a sign and send a specific message. Each of these basic clothing items is a sign. Once an item is assigned to "Punk," it becomes a signifier because it now has the idea or concept of "Punk" attached to it and that item has become the signified. Are your eyes closing yet? Stay with me as we explore the meanings of these pieces through another lens.

Rebel style

British fashion designer Keanan Duffty defines fashion as "the personal expression of our identities" (2009, p. 8) in his book *Rebel Rebel Anti-Style*, written with Paul Gorman. He continues by defining style as the choices each of us make daily in how we visually present ourselves (2009, p. 9). The book is a deep dive into eight key pieces of clothing that are consistently found in "the looks and styles of outsiders, musicians, artists, rebels and subcultures on the cutting edge of the visual arts" (2009, p. 8) that can broadly be categorized as rebel style.

Jeans: Blue jeans began their life as a sign of utility and hard work and this pretty much held through the Second World War. In the 1950s, jeans were co-opted by bikers, beats, and artists, and it wasn't long until they became legend in popular culture through James Dean and Elvis and embraced by hippies, mods, rockers, Punks, and hip-hop artists. Jeans are ubiquitous today and exist at every level of fashion (2009, pp. 18–19).

T-shirt: The T-shirt has its roots in nineteenth-century undergarments. Typically, a jersey knit made of cotton or cotton blends, the T-shirt transitioned into casual wear in the 1950s. They paired well with jeans and were adopted as a set by the many of the groups who wore them. Women began to adopt them in the 1960s. T-shirts provided the blank canvas for promotion, used by bands, movements, and designers alike (2009, pp. 32–33).

Combat Boots: According to a Wohlford Boots, Saving Soles blog post, counterculture groups in the 1960s and 1970s appropriated the military parade boot, a symbol of institutional power and conformity, as a symbol of rebellion and nonconformity. This is a lesson in subversion. When worn by other groups, the meaning of combat boots, generally considered a symbol of power and authority, is undermined and the power and authority is diminished. For Punks, the co-optation of the boots was an act of challenging the status quo. The combat boot earned iconic status in fashion via Punk Culture, and the combat boot continues to be a staple of Rebel Style today.

Boots were and still are well suited to Punk. They are protective at shows, especially if you are in or near the pit. They are good for walking, biking, or public transportation, which were and still are predominant ways we get around. AND you could kick and run in them if necessary.

As you can see, each of the key pieces can be assigned to various ideas or concepts, creating a highly nuanced language understood only by those who accept the same assignment. For example, a person who identifies as a biker would never mistake a Punk motorcycle jacket for a biker motorcycle jacket, and thus would not mistake a Punk for a biker. Style allows us to "advertise" our identity to those who speak the same identity language. It is one of the avenues we have at our disposal to help us find our tribe. As Judith Schaechter explains in a response to a questionnaire in 2009, *"It was like brand name recognition – I recognized my tribe by their feathers as it were. Not at all anymore – but back in the day."* In some ways this may be true, but Judith reports her uniform today is a Dockers skort, tights, and KEEN boots. It's not so far from back in the day. This outfit provides full-body coverage. It has utilitarian pockets useful for her craft and biking. And you've already heard about the importance of boots.

Acquiring and making your style

Vintage and thrift shop clothing was one of the foundations of any Punk's closet. In the early 1980s, you couldn't buy a "Punk" look at the mall, and even if you could buy it somewhere, you likely didn't have the money to spend. You had to work for it, build it yourself, and that was so great because you were able to create your own variation of the basics. There were lots of thrift shops and the finds were amazing. Not only could you get foundational pieces like jeans, T-shirts, and flannels, but also great quality leather jackets, men's blazers, women's fur coats and fur- and beaded-collar sweaters from the 1950s/1960s, some great women's pieces from the 1940s, and lots of shift dresses from the 1960s, sometimes even couture.

In the 1980s and early 1990s, much of the tribe's clothing was sourced at thrift shops, sale shops, and the local army surplus store. The reuse aesthetic speaks to limited money for new clothing all the time, interest in the history of a garment, concern for the environment, and the culture of consumption.

iGoldbergs, Philadelphia's original army and navy store, which operated from 1919 to 2019, was filled with useful and durable products for all sorts of work and leisure activities The basement was filled with authentic military surplus and exclusive heritage brands that offered great quality at affordable prices. It was our go-to shop for leather and military jackets, and boots. I scored my army boots there and they are still in my closet today.

Many of us could not go full-on Punk to work, but we carried our style with us removing total "Punk" designations from our dress and adopting mainstream designations that were less threatening and more office appropriate, resulting in a retro vibe, for example, a vintage dress, leopard-collar cardigan, and boots.

Fashion and Punk Culture

There is a tension between fashion and Punk Culture that Survey Respondent 17 describes in her 2007 response to a question about mainstream fashion from a 2007 questionnaire,

> *"I have a love/hate feeling about it. On one hand, it's a fun playground for ideas, artistic interpretations, having fun with the elements (color, fabric, shape, etc.), and I do get ideas*

from it or pick up on trends I like and find a low-cost version for myself. On the other hand, it's a greed-driven industry like any other, and part of the method for constant income for sellers of clothing/accessories is to prey on women's insecurities and make them want to keep refreshing their wardrobe because they can never be beautiful just as they are, but maybe that new dress they saw in Vogue will make them desirable."

Survey Respondent 17's commentary is well documented in marketing studies. In the 1977 edition of *Ways of Seeing*, essay #7, a book based on a BBC television program from the 1970s, John Berger and contributors discuss the message behind the "publicity image," a term used to describe the totality of visual sales messages we are subjected to every day. The group proposes that publicity is a language that offers the recipient choices which result in a single proposal.

> It proposes to each of us that we transform ourselves, or our lives, by buying something more. This more, it proposes, will make us in some way richer – even though we will be poorer for having spent our money. The method used by publicity to persuade us is to show us people who have been transformed by the purchase. It's not about the objects purchased, but rather the perception of social currency that those transformed are envied from the outside by others. (Berger et al., 1977, p. 131)

Rejecting corporate messaging

"Everything (vintage, new, work, casual, formal, coats, shoes, accessories) is from thrift stores. I do so for value as much

as for economic/environmental reasons – trying to be less of an 'American consumer' by purchasing used goods." – Survey Respondent 7, questionnaire response, 2007

Thrifting continues to be a primary channel for procuring clothing. I visit thrift and consignment shops regularly to buy, donate, and sell clothes. It's not uncommon for several of us to go out for an afternoon of group thrifting. Thrifting is a wonderful way to find outstanding pieces that make a memorable outfit. There are fewer thrift shops and far fewer fantastic finds. The best pieces are being bought up by vintage stores before they even make it to the thrift shop floor.

As we moved into the late 1990s and 2000s, clothing swaps became another avenue for procuring clothes. Every so often someone would host and we'd settle in for an afternoon of food, drink, and fun. Everyone would put their pile of clothes out and like sisters in a large extended family, we dove right in, squabbling for cool pieces, selecting specific pieces, and styling each other. Pleased with our new looks, we'd strut a makeshift catwalk for all to see, Punk performance at its most entertaining. The swapping of clothing revives the garment, allowing it to live a new life, styled in new and different ways, assigning a new and different meaning, but it also allows the new owner to keep a piece of the old owner, her sister/friend. When all was said and done, we'd pack up the leftovers and donate them to a women's shelter, passing them on to women in need, fulfilling our dedication to positive community activism.

Those of us who had better-paying jobs were able to afford pieces from fashion designers of the time: John Fluevog (distinctive, creative shoes), Betsey Johnson (unconventional fashion), and Stephen Sprouse (graffiti-inspired fashion) were big in the United States, while Vivienne Westwood was the godmother of Punk from the United Kingdom. Stores carrying contemporary designers in Philadelphia included Plage Tahiti and Mooshka in the luxury shopping district around Rittenhouse Square. Skins and Zipperhead, known for its Camden Town, London facade featuring sculptural ants crawling out of a zipper, offered Punk and new wave attire on South Street. Today, Survey Respondent 7, reports she *"is constantly scrolling Etsy and eBay for everything from basics to designer pieces, particularly those by vintage 80s designers."*

I was able to purchase some pieces by Norma Kamali, Betsey Johnson, and Kenzo in the early 1980s. I worked at Bloomingdale's and my employee discount plus the one-day sales discounts (thank you, Macy's) made them attainable. My biggest fashion regret was giving away my Norma Kamali, black and white buffalo check shirt dress, my Betsey Johnson thin-striped corset dress with puff sleeves, and my Kenzo three-piece knit suit. I did keep a Norma Kamali carpet bag, but the fabric handle failed, so I ended up donating it to the Drexel Costume Collection for student study.

Punk media – magazines, comics, and zines

Media helped Punks develop critical thinking skills. Just because a song got radio play didn't mean it was good. Music criticism and commentary provided information that presented a fuller picture of the movement, the genre, and the key players. The revered journalistic and critical voices, especially nationally, were decidedly male and often their arguments revolved around authenticity.

National Punk media

Because our group was centered around the music, many of us consumed local and national media. Music magazines, notably the recently revived (2022) *CREEM* magazine was originally launched in 1969 in Detroit, featuring pioneer rock music journalist and critic Lester Bangs, who offered witty and abrasive commentary on many genres of the evolving music scene. Like the music of the era, his style challenged and expanded the norms of music journalism. Respondent 7, a journalist, cites Bangs and Jack Kerouac (known as a leading writer of the Beat Generation, a youth subculture from the late 1950s) as the two writers who inspired her to become a journalist.

Likewise, *Trouser Press* magazine, founded in 1974, became the seminal publication of music journalism with a particular focus on Punk, new wave and alternative rock. Respondent 9, who grew up in the Poconos, recounted her first experience with *Trouser Press*. She was on THE iconic family cross-country road trip in the family station wagon to visit relatives. They stopped at a diner along the way and there was a wait for the table. She noticed a record store nearby and headed there to kill some time. She found *Trouser Press* and never looked back.

Zines

My journalist friend was also inspired by local and national zines (fanzines) that featured our contemporaries writing about and critiquing music, interviewing bands, and sharing commentary. They would have been considered the influencers of the time. The local zines were handmade and self-published (xeroxed) before that became a thing. They were creative outlets for individuals, groups, and communities to share their ideas, art, stories, and events. They were distributed for free at clubs and shows. National zines were often promoted in music catalogs or included with records, especially compilations. The Freedom Has No Bounds website has a comprehensive list of national and local zines and newsletters, including Beat Fete and Luna Ticks (featuring artwork by Elizabeth Fiend).

Developed from a Berkeley radio show in the late 1970s, *Maximumrocknroll*, aka Maximum rock 'n' roll, is one of the most recognized fanzines, the de facto newspaper of record for the Punk and hardcore scenes. Based in San Francisco, this not-for-profit monthly publication maintained a global focus. Published as a monthly into late 2019, each issue included artist interviews, music reviews, op-ed pieces, regular columns, and submissions from international contributors. With an over 30-year history, *Maximumrocknroll* became an establishment publication and that caused friction in a scene where once something becomes too well known, it's considered to have been co-opted and the scene will move on.

According to an article by Zoe Greenberg in the *Philadelphia Inquirer* dated May 4, 2024, "The Internet Is Over. Long Live the Zine." At least that is what the headline reads. Zines have existed since the invention of the printing press. They are ephemeral, noncommercial, and self-published (well before that was a thing). They often catalog cultures outside the mainstream, and that certainly was true for Punk. What could be more Punk than a DIY project that was produced and distributed for free?

Philadelphia has become home to numerous zine libraries and archives, collected, and housed by individuals, small collectives like Soapbox, a West Philly community print shop, and larger institutions like Temple University's Special Collections and Research Center. The Free Library of Philadelphia is starting its first zine collection. There's also a devoted community engaged by various events like the Philly Zine Fest, the West Philly Zine Fest, zine-making workshops, and zine swaps.

The article includes an interesting story from interviewee Kathie Haegele, who has been making zines since 2004:

> She met her husband at a New Jersey zine fest in 2009 and has made a host of zine friends over the years. One of them, a "long distance zine friend" named Vanessa Berry, will be visiting Haegele from Australia this fall. They've never met in person but have kept in touch by mailing zines back and forth.

This was one of the coolest things that happened in a pre-globalized, analog world. Instead of pen pal, one might have had a zine pal. Even if it wasn't a two-way human interaction, the idea that you could get a DIY international publication was amazing. Pre-digital, you would send cash in your homeland's currency to another country with different currency. The recipient would have to physically go to get your currency converted. It's a lot of work for the zine producer for very little payoff. Then the zine would have to be packed up and posted back. That would require a physical trip to the post office. In those days, international mail would take about two weeks between the United States and the United Kingdom. Today it averages five days from door-to-door.

Comics

Philadelphia has played an important role in political cartoons, as shown by the current exhibition at the Historical Society of Pennsylvania (HSP) located in Philadelphia. The exhibit is titled *Cartoons as Political Speech in Colonial and Contemporary America*. According to the website,

> This exhibit touches on Philadelphia's role in late colonial and Revolutionary politics, burgeoning publishing and print culture, and transatlantic commerce and communication. HSP's collection of political cartoons is a visually rich and interesting record of the struggle to form the new nation, the emergence of partisan politics, and the dynamic role of Philadelphia at the end of the 18th century.

Peter Crimmins reports for WHYY in an online article titled "Make Room for Cartoons among America's Founding Documents" that David Brigham, CEO of the HSP, stated, "Our founding story is one of feeling oppressed by a foreign power, or a power that's thousands of miles away, feeling that we don't have a voice at the center of power." These same feelings were the catalyst for Punk Culture.

Recent editorial cartoons by Signe Wilkinson are included in the exhibit. A Pulitzer Prize-winning cartoonist formerly for the *Philadelphia Daily News* and currently for the *Philadelphia Inquirer*, Wilkinson explores many facets of women's rights, public schools, trash, and public safety. But no matter the institution under fire, her cartoons are fundamentally about freedom of speech and that connects her to political cartoon history. "These are the founding principles and equality and censorship," Wilkinson said.

Punks continue to use cartoons to provide commentary on current political and institutional actions. Both Elizabeth Fiend and Judith Schaechter are two of the women in the Philly scene who created and published comics. Judith forged an alliance with other Philadelphia artists to form MissionCreep – alternative art, music, humor, stories, poetry, and so on – and parlayed her lifelong penchant for doodling and a dark, sarcastic sense of humor into a prolific series of artworks featured in Punk zines. Elizabeth, under the name Luna Ticks, created comics on her own, in the form of chapbooks, small paper booklets with one frame on a page. Recently, Elisabeth's comics experienced a small renaissance with the celebration of the fiftieth anniversary of *Weirdo*, an anthology of comics created by Robert Crumb (a nationally recognized Philadelphia cartoonist known for satirizing American culture), published from 1981 to 1993, and with the publication of the book *Tits & Clits 1972–1987*, in which she has a three-page comic and the distinction of having been censored by the comics publisher for her comic being "too disgusting," as told in the book's introduction. Elizabeth recounts her entire *Weirdo* experience in a self-published essay on her website, Slaw.me

Local Philly press

Free local papers, *City Paper*, *The Welcome Mat*, and *Philly Weekly*, always included shows in their "Happenings" sections. Even the

Philadelphia Inquirer, a serious paper of record, listed the shows in the Weekend section, a separate magazine devoted to current events in the city. Respondent 7 remembers seeing a listing for the Butthole Surfers in one! They used asterisks in the name, but still the listing was progressive for an esteemed publication.

4
Philly Punk music: "So much fun, I love KeN" profile: Marina D'Angelo, cofounder, KeN the band

"Music lets out my inner wild child. It lets me be an outsider but not an outcast." – Respondent #4, questionnaire response, 2007

A brief history of Philly music

Let's face it, there's a long history of music in Philadelphia. After all, Philly was one of the country's first cities, founded in 1682. Every genre since that founding has been featured there. Recently there has been a focus on Francis Johnson, a black composer and musician popular in the Revolutionary and antebellum eras. His story was part of an exhibition at the Museum of the American Revolution in Philadelphia titled *Black Founders: The Forten Family of Philadelphia*.

Francis Johnson was but one of many legendary artists who is part of the rich and diverse musical history of Philadelphia that has significantly influenced various genres.

In the early twentieth century, the city's music scene was dominated by jazz and blues, showcasing John Coltrane, Dizzy Gillespie, and others. The proximity between New York and Philly fostered an exchange of ideas and styles that coalesced into the innovative jazz and blues sounds that provided the foundation for the future.

The Philly sound, aka Philly soul

According to Chronicling America, Philadelphia became known for the Philadelphia sound, aka Philly Soul, in the 1960s and 7190s. Songwriting and production partners Kenneth Gamble and Leon Huff, aka Gamble and Huff, championed their signature sound featuring smooth melodies, orchestral arrangements, and soulful vocals that drew the attention of artists from many genres. Their label, Philadelphia International Records, produced numerous hits for The O'Jays, Harold Melvin & the Blue Notes, Teddy Pendergrass, and more.

Many Gamble and Huff productions were recorded at the famed Sigma Sound Studios. Established in 1968 by engineer Joe Tarsia, the studio's state-of-the-art facilities and talented engineers attracted a wide range of artists. Collaborating with Sigma and local musicians added a distinctive Philly Soul flavor that inspired the global music scene.

David Bowie, one of my favorite artists, was captivated by the Philly Soul sound, so much so that he recorded parts of his *Young Americans* album at Sigma Sound in 1974. I wish I had been just a bit older and lived in the city in 1974. I would have been a Sigma Kid. They were a group of Bowie fans who camped outside Sigma Sound Studios when Bowie arrived and they stayed until he finished. Bowie rewarded them with an invitation to hear the album first!

I'm jealous to this day, but I did get my own intimate Bowie/Sigma experience years later. The Sigma Sound Studios Collection, approximately 7,000 audio tapes of pop, soul, disco, and R & B recordings that became known as "The Sound of Philadelphia" was donated to the Drexel Audio Archives at Drexel University. I was teaching an Honors course about David Bowie and one of my colleagues mentioned the archive had the Bowie recordings. I was able to arrange a private listening event for my class. WOW! We got a real understanding of Bowie's process. He didn't tell the studio artists what he wanted done; rather, he guided them toward realizing the sound he was imagining. AMAZING!

Philly also played a significant role in the development of hip-hop, with pioneering West Philly artist Schoolly D. Philly's diverse musical heritage created a musical melting pot that fostered creativity and innovation that allowed different genres to thrive, intersect, and exist peacefully together.

Today, Philly continues to be a vibrant music city, supporting venues that present new and local talent through well-established global acts.

Select local record labels and studios late 1980–1990s

Independent record labels popped up on the scene focused on supporting local Punk bands, fostering a sense of community, and promoting Philadelphia's distinct Punk sound. As the scene evolved, new labels emerged to accommodate the diverse array of subgenres within Punk music. The following information was researched on Discogs.com.

Currently operating in San Francisco, Rave Records was founded in Philadelphia and released work by More Fiends, Pagan Babies, Flag of Democracy (F.O.D.), and Trained Attack Dogs

Buy Your Records, a New Jersey-based label that went out of business in 1990, released work by Electric Love Muffin and Flag of Democracy (F.O.D.)

Skyclad Records in Middlesex, New Jersey, released work by Sic Kidz, the Friggs, Pink Slip Daddy, and Dr. Bombay

Red Music was founded by Gino Wong and Richard Jordan in the late 1970s to release experimental music. They existed from roughly 1979 to 1984. They released work by early Philly bands like Ruin, The Stickmen, McRad, Executive Slacks, and Bunnydrums.

Studio Red is a recording studio founded in Old City Philadelphia by Adam Lasus in 1990. Now located in North Hollywood, California, bands including Caterpillar, Suffacox, and Madder Rose were recorded in Philadelphia, as reported by Sara Sherr in the *Philadelphia Weekly* on June 12, 1996.

Select local bands

The same holds true for local bands as for places: there are just too many to name. The overall Punk/hardcore band scene was predominantly male. I've introduced you to some of the regulars on my dance card: Trained Attack Dogs, Serial Killers, More Fiends, She Males, and Deadspot. Other local bands that we frequently saw included Homo Picnic, Pagan Babies, Scab Cadillac, and Electric Love Muffin.

What do all these bands have in common? You guessed it. Of those listed, More Fiends was THE ONE band with a woman, Elizabeth Fiend, on this list. This was not unique to Philadelphia. Elizabeth shared that in their two European tours, More Fiends only played once with a band that had a woman member. The 2008 fictitious account of the Philly Punk scene, *Broad Street* by Christine Weiser (a one-time bass player for the Philly girl band Mae Pang), reinforces the lack of women in bands early on in the scene. Protagonist Kit Green is mad at the men in her group for their callous treatment of women. She suggests that the women start a band, exclaiming "What better way to get back at these guys than to piss on their precious territory?" (Weiser, 2008).

"SO MUCH FUN, I LOVE KeN" – Marina D'Angelo, cofounder, and bassist of KeN

KeN was founded in 1995 by Marina D'Angelo and Bad Cop (band name), both fixtures on the scene before the founding of the band. In their words, they wanted to create a balls-out rocking girl band behind a male singer. They were reacting to the pigeonholing of female singers like Liz Phair and Sheryl Crowe. Women who rock hardly ever get their due, even today.

KeN's goal was to avoid objectification. KeN, like our micro scene group, is about the music. At its inception, the girls (their words) wanted the audience to think they were coming to see a male band and then find it was a group of hard-rocking women. The original band included all female musicians with chops, including Judith Schaechter. The original lead singer, KeN, was Marc

Beck, a Philly musician known for his various associations with Crankcase (whose members also founded Static Records, a Philly Label), the Heroics, Vick Logic, and his solo project, Revelogic.

Current members can't agree on a categorization of the band. All will say there are Punk rock influences in the sound, but from there the thoughts diverge. One thing that makes them stand apart from most other bands is their creative process. The band writes songs together as a group, rather than playing to offerings of individual members. Themes are generally dark – grief, loss, frustration, anger, disenchantment. Often sex is the euphemism. They certainly follow the DIY Punk tenet, from learning their métier to creating fliers, recordings, and performances.

Not all the current members of KeN identify as Punk; however, they all describe themselves as misfits or outcasts. Marina describes herself as "Always too smart to be cool and too cool to be smart."

KeN is an integral part of each member's life. To protect their privacy, they have requested I use their band names in this discussion. For KRS-10, it is the socializing and noisemaking. JennPie sees it as a creative outlet and vehicle for growth individually and as a band. Marina (band name Jiggle D'Jello) and Bad Cop are most connected to KeN. Perhaps this is because they have been there since the start. Marina states, "We ARE Ken," and Bad Cop describes KeN as "an invisible other. That odd twin." Most interestingly, drummer Devil Kitty reveals, "I have never fit in anywhere, except KeN and E Morto Cosi [his former band]." They have all bonded as eclectic friends, a Punk family.

Over the years, KeN has developed a hard-rocking girls reputation, leaving the original objective of KeN moot. JennPie has assumed the role of lead singer, and "Ken" is no longer the front man. He is firmly placed in the back behind the drum kit. Devil Kitty has a unique perspective on KeN.

Devil Kitty classifies KeN as a "girl band." He describes the music as "raw, angry, petty, mean and grimy with riffs that create unresolved tension." He continues,

> KeN is a gritty band with a shitload of attitude. I feel quite comfortable being in this band, a girl band. I don't have to stand up for anybody because anyone in KeN has a cool head but would rip yours off if pressed. [...] I do feel proud to be part of KeN.

JennPie describes the band's approach to performance succinctly, "There's always a theme when we play out, and through costume and performance, we are able to represent." The theme is generally derived from some rant or running joke, and the band has run the gamut from Goth to mad scientists to nuns.

KeN engages others, friends, and/or the audience in their performance. In true Punk fashion, Bad Cop says, "[We] just wing it and hope it all works out for the best." I had the honor of being part of a live performance at Yards Brewery (an early Philadelphia craft brewery that hit the big time). The band enlisted me and another of our friends to act as "ring girls" like they have in boxing matches to announce the round. Scantily clad beauties parade the ring holding up a poster with a number indicating the round on it. Our job was to parade down a walkway with the name of the next song on the poster. Now, I was not scantily clad, but I am sure I had a costume parodying the ring girl look and I am sure it likely included a wig.

On a rainy Sunday evening in April of 2023, KeN opened for another local band, The Donuts (a Philly garage band fronted by John Train), at Kung Fu Necktie. Situated under the Frankford El in Fishtown, Kung Fu Necktie is a dive bar that offers up plenty of live music in an intimate space with pretty good acoustics, and a great selection of beer. It was the first time many of our hyperlocal crew had been together since the pandemic. As ever with KeN, it was a fun show and that is why KeN is one of the girl bands in the city that has longevity.

The women and the music fall into the basic Punk tenets I have defined in this book. They are old-school Punks leading bricolage lifestyles. Three of the women are married and are moms with kids, and all of them have deep connections with their friends. The band follows a DIY process in their playing, writing, promoting, and performance. The band has clearly transformed over time, not only through a variety of members, but they have a proven record as women who rock. They no longer stand behind "KeN" as a front man to avoid objectification. The band and their music has transformed as the lives of the members and the members themselves have changed.

I can't end this profile about Marina without a jacket story, so here goes. Marina first met Judith Schaechter at a party in West Philly and recounts, "I knew when I saw her hair we would be friends." Not only did Judith have great hair, but she also had a white leather jacket. Marina coveted it and went on a quest to find her own. Her search finally ended at American Thrift at 8th and Wolf (right around the corner from my former 9th and Ritner Street home. I got some of the best stuff there.) Marina was proud of that jacket. It was an Evel Knievel (an American stunt performer known for his outrageous motorcycle jumps) style motorcycle jacket with a nice fit and a Nehru (a short stand-up) collar. It was a great fit and provided a protective layer for the pit and for riding a bike. In the early days, many of the crew traveled all over the city by bike. Marina caught the eye of her future husband with that white jacket. When the white leather died, her husband bought her a white Wrangler denim jacket because he couldn't find a cool white leather one. Marina wore the Wrangler until it fell apart and her husband replaced it again. He's also bought her white sunglasses and most recently white go-go boots. That reminds me that my ex arrived home from a tour with a pair of real white cowboy boots for me. I called them my Sally Starr (a celebrity television hostess in the 1950s and 1960s) boots and wore them a long time.

5
A celebration of failure, innovation, and success profile: Judith Schaechter, international stained glass artist

I think I first met Judith Schaechter in the early 1980s hanging around the keg in the backyard of a house party on Rodman Street (one of our regular South Street area spaces). Judith was memorable for many reasons, but what I most associate her with from this time was her white leather motorcycle jacket. It was a bold statement – a white beacon in a sea of black.

> *"I remember back in the punk days I loved the fashion but I was a bit more subdued – I had a leather motorcycle jacket and the de rigueur combat boots (still love those boots and wear 'em) but not the heavy duty studs and safety pins thing. No tattoos. A dorky punk look – not a scary punk look."* – Judith Schaechter, questionnaire response, 2009

Judith got the jacket at iGoldberg, our local army surplus store. White was different, she was one of only two people on the scene at the time who had a white jacket. She chose it because coming from RISD (Rhode Island School of Design), where all the girls dressed like Minnie Pearl (an America comedian, well known for her appearance on the popular television show *Hee Haw* from 1969 to 1991), she didn't feel she quite fit into the Philly Punk scene, which leaned hardcore when she arrived. White provided a level of intimidation and provided protective armor. It allowed her to be Punk adjacent on an island of misfit toys. Judith continued, *"I loved the punk rock look – to me it was super sexy. It was a signifier of someone who was interested in the same stuff as me – not just the music but in being transgressive culturally in general. Why that should be sexy beats me! Punk seemed smart."* – Judith Schaechter, questionnaire response, 2009.

My musings on the leather jacket

A leather jacket is a commitment. It is armor that envelopes you in a protective shell that is sturdy and heavy, hard to pierce. Just as a cat's or a dog's hairs go up to make them look bigger under threat, so too the leather jacket presents an intimidating image, which is often made more menacing with paintings and hardware embellishments.

My first leather jacket was a long-term loan from my friend who originally connected me to the scene. It was a black leather men's field coat with buttons up the front. It wasn't particularly intimidating, but it did turn out to be physically protective. While walking a few blocks from my apartment to the Gaskill Street house (a frequent meeting place) where my friend lived, I was jumped by a teenager with a knife. The protective layer provided by the coat gave me enough confidence to fight with less concern that I would be cut and I got away.

My second leather jacket was on loan from my ex-husband. We were dating at the time. He was an entertainer and left it with me while he was on tour. That jacket was a full-on UK Punk motorcycle jacket complete with painted back and many studs. It was aggressive and physically heavy, but it was truly protective. No one came near me. His jacket was his surrogate, his arms around me, protecting me while he was miles away.

During his tour, I flew out to meet him and took him his jacket. He was heading into a leg where he could hang out with some West Coast bands. The jacket was way too hard and heavy to pack, so I wore it. They'd never let me on a plane dressed like that today! I sat in a window seat, Walkman headphones on, Serial Killers Roadside Rendezvous playing. The gentleman seated next to me was surprisingly unphased. He waited until I took the headphones off for dinner and simply asked me if I was a rock star he should know. What a laugh!

My third leather jacket is MY leather jacket. It was given to me by my ex-husband, painted and studded by him for me. The featured band is NoMeansNo and the graphic is from the song "Dad." I love this jacket. It is a symbol of our relationship from start to finish. I have and will carry it with me to my end. It too is a commitment and I don't wear it often because it is physically heavy. If I don't wear it every day, my back aches. And in today's world, it is likely the jacket would draw the wrong kind of attention. What is notable about all three of these jackets is that they were given to me from two of the most important men in my life with whom I always felt safe.

Judith's creative work

In an interview in August 2009, I asked Judith about the influence of Punk on her life and creative work.

> I was very influenced by this movement [...] I really wanted to be part of it, although it was more or less over by the time I was in my early 20's in the 1980's. The "cool people" in my Jr High and High School – all of whom identified strongly with the Hippy Movement, had rejected me. It was natural for me to reject them back and the sort of willfully pissed-off, nihilistic and DIY aesthetic of punk made perfect sense to me. Pop music had become elaborate and baroque – impossible to aspire to. Punk was simple and messy – anyone could do it! Even me! Art of the 1980's followed the punk movement – at least in New York City until the art market crashed in the mid 1980's. The aesthetic was analogous – messy, fun, funny[...] nihilistic, cartoony, and bratty.

True to the US post-Punk music scene, Judith tried her hand at singing and guitar doing stints with local Philly bands Icebox and KeN, and participated in a collaborative project with musician Mark Beck, *Judith Schaechter Vs. Revelogic*.

> I wrote songs, and played guitar in all three and sang in Icebox and the collaborative. I took guitar lessons when I was around 14 years old – classical and flamenco for a couple of years in an attempt to learn to read music [...]

it didn't really take [...] the interest and patience weren't there.

Judith arrived on the Philly scene in 1983 as an emerging stained glass artist, self-taught. (She had taken one elective course in stained glass at RISD.) Left to her DIY devices, Judith trash-picked a window sash and purchased a kiln and light bulbs for about $70, then constructed her own light tables and tools when she moved into her first Philadelphia studio. Being creative, using these restraints was liberating. Judith has pushed the medium in a variety ways applying unconventional techniques, incorporating layering, engraving, collage, painting, photomechanical stenciling, sandblasting, and digital technology in the process as she creates her elaborate pieces. There was room for innovation in stained glass as a medium that had traditionally been mostly Gothic or Tiffany.

Judith's process

Judith explains how she makes a stained glass window:

> I use a material called "Flash Glass". Flash glass is a type of glass with a paper-thin veneer of intense color on a base layer of lighter color.
> First, I cut the glass using a steel wheel cutter and a grozing or running pliers. The next step is sandblasting. This is a process by which one can remove the colored layer, sometimes in stages to get patterns and tones. After sandblasting, I engrave smaller details using a flexible shaft engraver. I also use diamond files to make smooth variations in the color.

The only paint I use is black. This fires onto glass at 1212° F. I usually do 2–5 firings as that is the best way to get rich blacks and grays. Sometimes I also use silverstain (which is yellow). This is all the paint I use – all the other color is the flash glass.

One reason there is a lot of color in each section of my pictures is that the flash glass is layered – sometimes up to 5 pieces deep.

Bricolage and nihilism

While Judith's process demonstrates two key elements of Punk – DIY and transformation – her finished pieces resonate aesthetically with bricolage and nihilism. Every work includes a bricolage of design motifs. Judith's work is often described as dark; however, Schaechter says of her formative years, "I just was morose and depressed […] So yes – those early experiences could well have channeled me into a nihilistic puberty […] and hence, punk." She continues to discuss the "darker" themes in her work, saying, "I also strongly believe that one must feel all their feelings as fully as they can and not repress the dark and/or 'ugly' thoughts (but not necessarily ACT on them!!)." While Judith's themes may be dark, there is another important attribute to her work, Beauty. It prompts the viewer's aesthetic response through the senses. It's visceral and sensual. It wakes you up and tugs at your emotions. For Judith, Beauty + Creativity + Inspiration is powerful.

"My mom was very psychological – in touch with some deep stuff in herself and encouraged me to be the same. She was very dark […] but very, very funny. Maybe she was punk, in her own way." Judith discusses her view on family,

> I am close to my family but I don't feel all that intimate with them – especially not compared to my closest friends. I have about six very close friends without whom I would be living an impoverished and lonely existence. They are truly family to me, yes.

As Judith and I discussed Punk in relation to our collective lives and creative works, we came to consensus – perhaps the most important legacy of the early Punk movement is the tenet to embrace failure. Fail spectacularly – the bigger and grander and wider the audience, the better. Learn from that failure and rise from the ashes like a phoenix to try again another day. Without failure, one cannot attain success. And you can't embrace DIY if you can't accept failure.

Ask Johnny Lydon (aka Johnny Rotten of the Sex Pistols) or the Ramones (a NYC Punk band formed in 1974) and a bevy of other Punk and post-Punk artists whose rise and fall are documented in the astutely titled *Rip It Up and Start Again* by Simon Reynolds, published by Penguin Books in 2006. Reynolds argues and documents not only the rise and fall of Punk music through a variety of bands, but he also analyzes the rise and fall of the post-Punk era, which he defines as 1978–1984. It is important to note that his dates of Punk from 1974 to 1977 and post-Punk from 1978 to 1984 mark the era of Punk and post-Punk music, not Punk Culture, which as the author maintains continues to this day (Reynolds, 2006).

Tech practitioners are encouraged to fail fast. This is the best legacy the tech industry had given to mainstream culture, the idea of embracing failure. Several books on the topic have been published, including *Celebrating Failure: The Power of Taking Risks, Making Mistakes, and Thinking Big, The Power of Taking Risks, Making Mistakes, and Thinking Big,* by Ralph Heath. Published by Career Press of Franklin Lake, New Jersey, in 2009, Heath takes a Punk approach to his self-help tome. Short chapters, like the infamous one-minute Punk song, barrage the reader with a single concept, short and sweet. Heath believes in the greatness of failure and opens the book with the following statement, "Failure and defeat are life's greatest teachers" (Heath, 2009). Each chapter features a callout titled "The Failure Factor," which features the concept behind the message of that chapter. His most "Punk" suggestions include Embrace new ideas and change, Live outside your comfort zone, Expect some pain, Swim against the current, Take action, and Keep moving. These titles pretty much sum up Punk in a nutshell.

None of this is to say that Judith is or has ever been a failure. In fact, she is an internationally renowned and collected artist with work in prominent institutions and private collections. She has had nothing but a successful career; however, she has attained success by embracing failure along the way.

6
Eat more veggies profile: Elizabeth Fiend, Change Agent

What do a librarian; an AFSME labor union steward and executive board member; a television show program host; a celebrity judge; a wedding officiant; a film/video creator, producer, and writer; an author, a journalist, an illustrator, and a slide guitarist have in common? They are the many facets of activist Elizabeth Fiend.

I first met Elizabeth Fiend in 1985 or 1986 when her band, More Fiends, were playing a show on the roof of the garage at Drexel University. I was in the audience wearing a thrifted 1960s shift dress in a red-orange and yellow-green allover geometric print, an orange chiffon scarf on my head, and my surplus US Army boots. This was a quintessential uniform for women on the Philly Punk scene. In fact, Elizabeth was wearing a similar version of the same outfit, although she may have been wearing a shift-style nightgown instead of a dress. Elizabeth often trolled sleepwear departments for her looks. At the end of the set, she spoke to a mutual friend and said, "I have to meet that girl in the red and green dress." We were promptly introduced and have been friends ever since.

I was wondering how I could kill a few hours while on a recent trip to Pensacola, Florida. A neighbor suggested that I should check out the thrift shop scene. It was a good call. It was likely there would be some good finds. I was thinking I just might find some 1960s dresses in Florida. A Google search showed there are many consignment, thrift, and antique stores in Pensacola. I got a recommendation from the person who had hired me and her guidance did not disappoint. I went to the "antique row" section of town, a strip of roadway with one antique store after another. The stores at the beginning did not look promising. I pulled over to figure out how to get to my hotel. It required me to make a left turn taking me across a very busy four-lane highway. It was going to be easier to proceed in the same direction I was going and use the center lane to go into a parking lot. That's what I did and my drive brought me to the Rusty Relic. It had a real retro vibe and some nostalgic outdoor furniture and décor, a promising indicator of what might be inside. I parked, walked inside, and was immediately rewarded with a dress form featuring a colorful floral print sheath dress, reminiscent of the 1960s–early 1970s. I could tell it had never been washed. I could still feel the finishes on the fabric. I checked the tag – vintage, but more like the 1980s–1990s. I determined this because the fabric includes stretch but the tag is old-school factory style. I checked the size – my size. I checked the price tag – $6! Mine! It's a fabulous psychedelic-style large-scale floral print in various shades of pink, red, and red violet, offset by bright orange and white. A Google search of the brand J. W. Treci resulted in lots of pre-owned garments that look to be a moderate clothing brand with sizing for misses, petites, and plus sizes, further evidence it was likely popular in the 1980s and 1990s, There is even a listing for the same dress on eBay, described by the quinchethorn account as *J W TRECI PINK FLORAL ALOHA PRINT BARB CORE 60'S STRETCH SHIFT DRESS*. The asking price is $13.99 or best offer plus $8.99 for shipping. I got a steal. I would have been lucky to find it for $20 in Philly. Add a moto jacket and some boots – work-ready Philly Punk style, same as it ever was.

Elizabeth fits the definition of old-school Punk. She has been on the scene since the late 1970s, continues to sport a Punk aesthetic, is employed as a university librarian (holding a BA in Art History), and participates in the music scene. Elizabeth entered college in the late 1970s where she met her soulmate, partner, and husband, Allen Fiend. They bonded quickly and have been together ever since, recently celebrating their fortieth wedding anniversary.

Feeling the music

For 15 years, Elizabeth played slide guitar for the Philadelphia-based psychedelic Punk band More Fiends, the first Philadelphia band to record a Peel Session for the BBC Radio in England. More Fiends toured America and Europe, and recorded two albums and six singles, either self-released or released on Rave, Semaphore, or other labels.

Live Punk music is a full-on assault on all five of your senses. Your ears are barraged. It is loud, sometimes ear bleedingly loud. It is a wall of sound that you feel through your entire body. Dress, stance, and movement of the performers set the attitude. And then there is the pit, a mostly controlled form of tribal dance. The collective movement of the audience from the pit to the stage divers to the dancers and spectators on the edge, coalesces in a physical connection and emotional relationship with the performers and audience who become one in energy and spectacle. Now those of you who are counting will point out that I have only referenced three senses. True, but all that physical activity results in a lot of sweating and sloshing around of beer. This provides the smell and believe me, licking sweat and sometimes beer as it pours down your face certainly hits taste.

Family, both biological and Punk

Many of the friendships Elizabeth has today were born on the Philly scene during these years with Elizabeth playing the roles of both performer and audience participant. Elizabeth stated that she views her friends as her family and surmises this may be because she has chosen not to have children (a choice made by a fair share of women in my micro Philly scene). Different from some Punks, however, she is also close to her and to Allen's biological family. Her friend circle includes a number of 40-year relationships, but Elizabeth is constantly making friends and she likes to have a lot of friends. The influx of new friends brings new interests, ideas, and growth, in essence transformation, one of the integral elements of Punk.

Personal style

Elizabeth sports a uniquely personal Punk aesthetic style that focuses on deconstructing class and gender and challenging the traditional view of woman as sexual object. Elizabeth believes that mainstream fashion is "driven by airheads and heiresses."

She described her dress as "clownish" and professed that she has always dressed this way. Her rationale is that her personal style is comfortable and reflects her identity – I AM ME. True to form, Elizabeth is ahead of the curve. The #003 edition of *Creem* magazine, the Spring 2023 issue, includes Leah Mandel's article entitled "Eleganza: The Big Ha! Clowncore is more than just the next strange trend in music and fashion – it's a lifestyle."

There are a lot of academic theories about women's fashion and Punk. Some say it was a reaction to fashion's presentation of conventional beauty, perfection, good taste, and wholesomeness. Others suggest that it was a subversive action to expose the mainstream society to marginalized groups like sex workers and those who practice deviant sexual behaviors. *Punk Style: Articles of Interest #6*, suggests that the self-taught Vivienne Westwood, who included the signs of deviant sexual behaviors in an early version of her King's Road store, Sex, went on to produce anti-fashion establishment clothing that had a beauty of its own. While her garments were expensive, her techniques and aesthetics were achievable through DIY. Her Punk look was co-opted by other designers and adopted by the masses.

As Don Letts said on the podcast *Punk Style: Articles of Interest #6*, the United States gave us Punk music and London gave us Punk style. That stereotypical London Punk man dated a London Punk woman who typically chose a style that celebrated flashy, cheap, and tacky, an over-the-top version of the stereotypical archetype of a South Philadelphia woman from the 1980s, albeit the result was quite different. The South Philly archetype was akin to Peg Bundy (the mom on the 1987–1997 American sitcom *Married with Children*).

Elizabeth has never met a project she can't tackle. Her learning process begins with research and reading. The next step includes a series of trials that may or may not be successful. Failure is not seen as a negative, but rather a learning experience. Elizabeth is not afraid to try nonconventional methods. For example, Elizabeth stated that she would feed fabric through a sewing machine with her left hand if that worked better for her than the recommended right hand. She believes this use of personalized, rather than conventional methods brings another level of interest to her final product.

The path to Punk

Elizabeth's journey began well before Punk hit the scene. A suburban child, Elizabeth participated in activities that instilled in her and fostered a strong sense of personal social responsibility that became a substantive part of her personal ideology. From shopping for shut-in seniors on food stamps, to participating in 4H projects, to taking summer classes in photography and other topics of interest, to looking at art books in the library, young Elizabeth practiced bricolage early on and as a young adult. Involvement in these pursuits allowed her to develop a strong sense of self-confidence, capability, and faith in her ability to problem solve and effect change. Punk was what she had been waiting for; it allowed her to assimilate all these experiences into "me."

Broadcasting a message

Embracing change has allowed her to share her tenet of social responsibility through music, art, and educational video. Elizabeth produced content to pursue her roles as activist and change agent under the umbrella of a project titled Big Tea Party. During the Big Tea Party years, Elizabeth created a series of three-minute videos for public television that were used as transitions between programs. Public television did not air commercials, so these three-minute messages acted as the bridge and space fillers between programs. One episode in 1998 features her forward-thinking recipe for a vegetarian cheesesteak, The Cheese Fake. The recipe is included in *Lonely Planet*'s travel guide *Philadelphia & the Pennsylvania Dutch Country* and as the only non-meat recipe in *The Great Philly Cheesesteak Book* (FYI by Carolyn Wyman). She gained widespread recognition and celebrity through this project and had opportunities to spread her message to larger audiences through associations with the Philadelphia Film Festival, *National Geographic*, *Traveler's Magazine*, and as a guest on NBC's *Today* show, and the Food Network's show *Roker on the Road*. But Elizabeth never wanted to be famous. Going bigger was hard work with a small payout and little effect.

Judged by the company you don't keep

Concurrently, the political Tea Party movement was gaining notoriety. Including libertarians, right-wing populists, and conservative activists, the movement hid elite interests behind a facade of grassroots development. Unfortunately, the Big Tea Party often got conflated with the political movement and this made it difficult for Elizabeth to find opportunities. Elizabeth rebranded with a new web presence, Slaw.me, but it was grueling to regain the reach of Big Tea Party during the rise of social media.

A parade provides a platform

Always up for the new, Elizabeth embarked on her life as a mummer in 2011. The mummers are a storied Philadelphia tradition, best known for the annual Mummer's Parade on New Year's Day. The oldest continuous folk parade in the United States has been formally sponsored by the city since 1901. Mummery, found in many cultures from ancient Egypt, to Greece, to Europe, found its way to Philadelphia in the seventeenth century with the influx of British and Scandinavian immigrants. It began as a "mum" through the neighborhood where small groups would offer up a performance in return for food and drink. The groups grew and organized into clubs that participate in one of five Divisions: The Comic, The Fancy, the Wench Brigade, the String Band, and the Fancy Brigade Divisions.

The spirit of mummery is a celebration of family and fun grounded in values and tradition. The event is filled with music, struts (a specific mummer dance), satire, political commentary, and lots of colorful costumes. Historically, clubs were organized around neighborhoods that supported the clubs through building props, sewing costumes, and fundraising. Many clubhouses were and are located on South 2nd Street. Affectionately known as 2 Street, the public post-parade party happens here.

I LOVE the Mummers. When I was married, we lived at 9th and Ritner Street, directly in the path of one of the largest comic brigades to the parade's starting point. Every New Year's Day morning, the Froggy Carr's wench brigade, an outrageous mega club marched from its 3rd Street clubhouse south to 3rd and Ritner where they serenaded their founder, James "Froggy" Carr, before the start of the parade. By the time they got to my house at about 7:30 a.m., they had to stop to get everyone back together. It was quite a scene to wake up to each new year, drunken wenches and residents in pajamas. My ex and I hosted a New Year's Day party and we'd all head to Broad Street to watch the parade, especially the string bands. When we had had our fill, we'd pack up the party and head over to my friends' house at 2nd and Watkins for the after-party and participate in the spectacle. Our 2 Street tradition continued for many years, surviving my divorce and our friends' move from Watkins Street to the suburbs. Another friend who had participated in our event for many years got a small first floor apartment on 2 Street and later moved to a larger 3rd floor apartment next door. He carried on the party tradition for many years.

In 2011, the city pushed the Mummers to professionalize, self-regulate, and make a concerted effort to become more inclusive in their membership and more culturally sensitive in their performances. That is when Elizabeth and Allen joined some of our other friends and formed a group called the Philadelphia Pranking Authority, a take on the infamous Philadelphia Parking Authority, subject of the popular A&E television program *Parking Wars* that aired from 2008 to 2012. Falling under the umbrella of the larger group of Landy Comics, Elizabeth took on a role as cocaptain. Elizabeth uses the parade as a platform for her "Eat More Vegetables" campaign. Their club membership is inclusive and has grown to about 40 people. (You must have 22 people to be on television.) Each year they pick a theme, pay their $15 dues, make their own costumes, and parade. It's the low-key end to mummery. At the "ALL IN" level, the Fancy Brigades present full-on mini theater productions at the convention center that they work on all year.

It is Elizabeth's Punk ideology that ultimately allows her to practice activism and effect change through a variety of DIY projects. Her varied roles demonstrate a bricolage of interests, held together by a common thread of connections that are uniquely her own. The breadths of projects show growth and transformation in Elizabeth the adult. Each role has been a DIY journey of research, process, and product that ties into her activism and faith and belief in social responsibility. As Elizabeth stated on the defunct Big Tea Party website, her "goal is to promote a sustainable living trinity – good health, environmentalism, and community activism, a practical, rewarding lifestyle where one's actions won't have negative effect on future generations."

And of course, Elizabeth has a jacket story too. Her jacket that had a More Fiends spiral painted on the back attracted a stalker. As she biked from West Philly to Center City, she noticed a woman on a bike frequently following her. Later, she came to know her stalker. It turned out to be JoAnn Rogan from the Philly band Thorazine.

Elizabeth achieved national distinction for another garment. Her hand-painted dress is part of the *American Punk* exhibit at the Rock a& Roll Hall of Fame Museum. The black and white dress features the More Fiends spiral symbol on the front and a skeleton on the back.

What's next for Elizabeth? Well, there's that science fiction story she started and never finished. Now that she is retired, maybe she'll get back to it.

7
"We are we": A reflection

More noteworthy women integral to the Philly Punk community

Kathy "Mom" Hughes is an influential figure in the Philly Punk scene. Many of us met her during her stint as bartender at Silk City, a retro cool bar and diner in the Northern Liberties section of Philadelphia. Known as the original "Tattooed Mom," Kathy has a long history of supporting artists. She fed and gave shelter to many bands traveling through Philadelphia and to community members in need. Kathy's family had a carnival, and in the off-season Kathy often had access to leftover food that she generously shared. In the 1990s, she opened Sugar Moms, a dive bar in the basement of a sugar refinery that had been turned into lofts in the gentrifying Old City. Her carnival roots shined through. The space was liberally decorated with carnival relics. Later, Kathy partnered with Robert Perry to open Tattoed Mom, on South Street, a bar that continues to be a testament to her legacy, supporting local and international talent and providing spaces where all are welcome. Kathy's influence and connections with the Philly scene remain strong. Four paste-up works by Elizabeth

Fiend now grace TMom's, Philadelphia's unofficial Street Art Museum, second floor ceiling as part of a June 2024 show/installation titled, "Now I Want to Sniff Some Glue." Described as

> our first ever wheat paste show & THE event for wheat paste artists to meet, exchange ideas & share their love for the art form. The show celebrates the international community that pastes on the streets and reaches out to artists all over the world to show their paste up art in all mediums on our walls, ceilings, doors, and floors of Tattooed Mom!

I was acquainted with Kathy through the larger scene and mostly interacted with her as part of a group, but there was one time when she "mommed" me. I was at a Bad Brains (a DC band that fused Punk, hardcore and reggae into a unique sound) show at Revival in Old City Philadelphia, a bar and music venue in what was originally built as a bank in the1830s. The bank facade remained, but the space inside changed over time, and in the Revival years there were two large-scale performance and dance spaces complete with bars, and some more intimate lounges and bars sandwiched in between. Bad Brains were popular in Philly. They always drew a huge crowd and this show was no exception. At one point, the entire crowd was engulfed by the pit and I found myself crushed into one of the massive support columns to the point where I was gasping for breath and thought I might pass out. Fortunately, the pit shifted just in time and I was able to move. I went directly outside for air and there on the step was Kathy. She asked me if I was OK and invited me to sit with her. I did. We sat together long after I regained my breath, chatting about everything and nothing until the show was over.

Beth Anne Lehman, credited as B.A.L. Stack, keyboardist from the Philly band Stick Men, was part of Elizabeth Fiend's first group of Punk friends in the late 1970s–early 1980s. At that time the Punk scene was very small and very underground. Punks really stood out and were shocking to the predominant culture. The Stick Men house in West Philly became party central, offering up Warhol-esque FUN to about 50 people on the regular. (Andy Warhol hosted parties in his factories that attracted the 1960s avant-garde.) Elizabeth describes Beth as a wonderful person, talented and funny. She behaved a lot like Lucille Ball in *I Love Lucy* complete with eye rolls, screeching, and laughter. She wanted to get married and she did, spending most of her adult life in the suburbs until her recent death from lung cancer. Elizabeth recounted that Beth had a 1950s green glittery dress that she wore at every show. Ironically, Elizabeth showed up to a party or show in the same dress made of a different fabric, one of many examples of a female relationship solidified by a garment.

Carol L. Schutzbank, musician, editor, writer, promoter, manager, salesperson, and friend. Upon her death in 1995, MTV described her as "Co-founder and senior editor of the internationally distributed seminal East Coast fanzine, *B-Side* […] and a prime mover on the Philadelphia underground rock scene booking local clubs, managing groups" (MTV News Staff, 1995).

Margit Detwiler recounts in a *City Paper* tribute that while studying journalism at Temple University, Schutzbank's music journey began as a keyboardist and singer in the band Initial Attack. She went on to book bands at the Kennel Club, worked at Pulsations nightclub, and managed bands including Scram, Ruin, and Electric Love Muffin (Detweiler, 1995).

Although she was well known and respected in music circles nationally and locally, she was Philly through and through, tirelessly working to get the Philly scene recognized on the world stage. In 1989, she and partner Karen McVicker cofounded Earwig – described in a *City Paper* cover story as "a music resource organization dedicated to the support and perpetuation of progressive and aggressive music in Philadelphia" (Detweiler, 1995).

In 1989, she became the Philly correspondent for *Big Shout Magazine* with a monthly feature, "Olio." (*Big Shout Magazine* was a monthly entertainment tabloid that covered the arts, issues, and entertainment in the Delaware Valley from March 1989 to June 1996.) In 1992, she joined the Delaware Valley Music Poll Awards, where she took on a leadership role in ceremony planning. Her health began to fail in the run-up to the fourth annual ceremony to be held at the Trocadero. She was unable to attend and wear the dress she had bought for the event. She passed away a couple of days after. Her family celebrated her determination and buried her in that dress (Kirk, 1995).

Nancy Barile, scenester and promoter for Sadistic Exploits, an early Philadelphia hardcore band known for organizing several Punk festivals in the early 1980s. In a Dan Gross 2020 interview for the website No Echo, Barile discussed her book *I'm Not Holding Your Coat*, a first-person account of the Philly Punk rock scene in the 1970s and 1980s.

Speaking about women on the Philly scene, Barile recounts,

> But my experience was that as a woman, it was super empowering. And so, a lot of that had to do with Philadelphia. Philadelphia was a really open-minded,

accepting place, you know, and there were a lot of strong females in that scene. And so, we fed off of each other. And then the men were respectful and protective, and fun to be around. And so, you know, I was very lucky in that. It definitely empowered me as a woman more than anything. Because we were up front, and we were on the stages, and we were behind the scenes, and we were managing the bands or writing the fanzines. And we were there. We were smaller in number, but we were mighty. (Barile, 2020)

Common threads

"The things that differ tend to be money related – like the 'status' level of their job, the amount of money they make, etc. We range a lot in this regard, though no one really cares or uses it as a definition of any kind." – Respondent 7, questionnaire response, 2007

There are so many common threads between Judith, Elizabeth, Marina, and me (and many of the other women in our group). Each of us four are college graduates with secondary degrees. Each of us works and/or worked in the university system. Each of us are creative content producers. Each of us is committed to educating others. Each of us practices DIY and is somewhat self-taught and is not afraid to try and fail. We are unconventional women who traverse the world in unconventional ways.

Overall, the larger group continues to share common attitudes, beliefs, and ideas. We continue to live unconventional lives. A good number of us live within a mile or two of each other and the rest a short drive or ride away. We are family at our foundation, friends for life, and provide the community necessary to continue to have a rich, full life as we age.

Have you noticed the importance of clothing and dress in our relationships? Not only was dress a tribal code, but it has been a key factor in the development of long and deep relationships. It was the attraction that launched lifelong friendships between Elizabeth and me, Judith and me, Marina and Judith, and Marina and her husband. The leather jacket holds so many deeply personal expressions and connections, it is almost a true second skin.

What happened to subcultures and subcultural style?

For many years, my fellow scholars and I would wonder where did subcultural style go? Cosplay, Comic Con, and Furries dress in costumes that mark their identification with certain characters or fictional worlds. There are subcultures online in gaming communities, groups that coalesce around particular games or genres and speak to each other in gaming language, but they do not necessarily have a clothing style.

As more and more people live their lives online, fed more of what they like through algorithms, we have grown into a society that has less and less shared cultural experiences. We choose what we consume and it may or may not be what our friends and acquaintances choose. There is very little cultural product left that crosses wide swaths of the population. Professional and collegiate sports and some big-time entertainers like Taylor Swift are a few examples that do. In this case the audience of one has resulted in the decline of real-life youth subcultures.

In a February 21, 2024, *New York Times Magazine* article titled "Teen Subcultures Are Fading. Pity the Poor Kids," author Mereille Silkoff, a raver in her youth, discusses subcultures in her day,

> Getting into a scene could be work; it required figuring out whom to talk to, or where to go, and maybe hanging awkwardly around a record store or nightclub or street corner until you got scooped up by whatever was happening. But at its deepest, a subculture could allow a given club kid, headbanger or punk to live in a communal container from the moment she woke up to the moment she went to bed.

A youth subculture she asserts, "affected almost everything you did: how you spoke, the way you dressed, the people you hung out with, the places you went, the issues you cared about."

She goes on to describe today's subculture as

> a hyperactive landscape of so-called aesthetics – thousands of them, […] These are more like cultural atmospheres, performed mainly online, with names and looks and hashtags, an easy visual pablum. They come and go and blend and break apart like clouds in the wind, many within weeks of appearing. They have much content but little context – a lot to look at but a very thin relationship to any "real life" anything, like behaviors or gathering places […] the real world cultural community that has been replaced by an algorithmic fluidity in which nothing hangs around long enough to grow roots.

It is estimated that the average time per day spent with digital media in the United States will be about eight hours by 2025. The sheer volume of digital imagery that assaults each of us daily has disrupted our ability to connect these aesthetics, made up of random things that could go together, to real-life experiences with profuse social meaning. The surrender to digital image has taken away the opportunity to be engulfed in a rich, five senses engaging subcultural experience. The surrender to digital interaction has impeded the ability for younger generations to identify the nuance of physical presentation. The surrender to the visual has taken away the highly specific language of subcultures. All that is left is an Instagram image with a hashtag that may or may not accurately reflect the visual cues in the image.

Subcultures aren't really dead. They are just not available to the masses who spend most of their time in their digital bubble. They are not even underground. They are there for the experiencing in the real-life places that provide a meeting space for the group. For those who want to put in the work, subcultures are available.

Another youth rebellion in fashion

I am pleased to see there is a current youth rebellion in fashion as reported in *The Guardian* on Tuesday, June 25, 2024, in an article titled "Dressing Pretty Is Over: This Is Fashion's Ugly Decade," by Hannah Marriot. In the article, Sean Monahan, a respected trend forecaster has been tracking the fashion movement since 2021. Daniel Rodgers, digital fashion writer for *British Vogue*, describes the current trend as nihilistic, sampling from various subcultures without the "lifestyle obligations" that used to be part of wearing those clothes. While it seems to be grounded in aesthetics, as discussed above, it does appear to be a rebellion against a decade of mass-produced athleisure and the "clean girl" look that many influencers "sell." Visually it is messy, drawing from Punk, Goth and grunge, a cherry-picked, DIY anti-fashion fashion.

Being Punk in a digital world

Today, everyone can and does participate in digital cultural production. Punk Culture is no exception. With DIY content production and distribution at its very core, Punk easily adapted to technology. Using new tools and platforms, it became easier to self-publish and distribute everything from music to zines to art. Email, forums, discussion boards and newsletters made it easy to communicate and connect with individuals and groups for various purposes. Punk cultural content production is a reminder that authenticity and innovation are more important than commercial success. With a commitment to social commentary and a willingness to speak out against injustice and oppression, it's the message that matters far more than the medium.

There is a nine-year difference in age span between the respondents to my original questionnaire of 2007. That puts us on a generational cusp (a person born during the last few days of one zodiac sign and the first few days of the next sign is said to be on the cusp, resulting in traits from both signs), as I like to think of it. I (no surprise), and we are betwixt and between the baby boomers and Generation X. Personally, I have never felt connected to either of them.

I've been thinking about generational groups all my professional life. Since the late 1980s, marketing has revolved more and more around highly sophisticated profiles of consumers. Today, we have arrived at the audience of one who demands highly curated collections of products they will love from their favorite brands.

My research and experience have led me to believe that the overlap between every two generations creates about a ten-year span of "tweeners," who are slightly different, betwixt and between. I was so satisfied when *VIEW* magazine (a trend publication created by the London-based trend forecasting service Viewpoint) described my group as Generation Flex sometime around the 2010s. They were dead-on. We were too old to be digital natives, but we were easily able to adapt to the rapidly changing digital world.

Many Gen Flexers were the first group of developers and designers of digital media. I was part of this group too. I taught myself how to design websites through information on AOL and did a ten-year stint consulting as a website designer, developer, and trainer. My company was called SmartLynx and I had some big clients including Motorola. I was part of PANMA, the Philadelphia Area New Media Association. It began as CyberSuds, a loose group of independents who met up for a beer once a month. While I was respected for my brain, it was a male-dominated industry, but as with the Philly Punk scene, these men accepted us as equals.

My role was the "It" girl (a young woman who has achieved celebrity because of her socialite lifestyle). I generally closed the happy hour and organized the after-party. This slice of New Media time was closely aligned with my Punk ethos – we were all independents. Many people (me) were self-taught designers and/or coders. Products or services were rolled out while we were still learning. There was a great community of helping, making referrals, and giving back. They were fun and heady times and we resisted joining the establishment until we needed them to take the next step after the dot-com bubble burst in 2000. Welcome back, misogyny.

Punk music still swimming against the tide

I was delighted to see this May 3, 2024, *Washington Post* headline: "The Most Popular, Obscure, Democratic, Republican & Hated Music in America." Andrew Van Dam and Travis Chase analyzed a YouGov survey Music and the Music Industry, conducted April 20–May 2, 2023, sampling 1,000 US adult citizens. I am proud to report Punk music is the only genre to achieve a negative approval rating! The analysts aptly report, "Which, honestly, probably sounds like a badge of honor." They go on to disclose, "But really, punk comes out on top overall only because anti-mohawk sentiment crosses party lines." And further, perhaps not so surprisingly, "Punk is the worst-rated genre in the South."

I'm sure this is not surprising to anyone who understands Punk. By definition, it and its messaging are culturally disruptive and politically antiestablishment. In recent times you might associate Punk with anarchists, antifa, far-left liberals, and libertarians. You might find it interesting, however, to note that a small collection of Punk musicians, including Johnny Ramone, are political conservatives. Johnny Ramone "came out" at the 2002 induction of the Ramones into the Rock & Roll Hall of Fame.

You may also find it interesting that according to Ben Jacobs, in a May 20, 2022, *Politico* article titled "How Gen X Became the

Trumpiest Generation," GenX is accepted as those born between 1965 and 1980. The oldest of this generation grew up under Ronald Reagan and the end of the Cold War. They would have first voted in the 1984 election between Reagan and Walter Mondale. Musically they gave us grunge and gangsta. They were depicted as slackers and considered apolitical. Those born in the mid- to late 1960s are predominantly Republican. In fact, white voters from this group are more conservative than the older boomers and the Silent Generation according to a model from 2014. Culturally, they leaned right, as demonstrated by the Michael J. Fox character Alex P. Keaton, the Reagan-loving teenager in *Family Ties*, a popular sitcom where Alex continually battled with his liberal boomer parents.

According to Republican pollster Kristen Soltis Anderson, those who cast their first votes in the Reagan, George H. W. Bush, and Bill Clinton elections were likely to lean right, and interestingly, most people continue to vote as they voted in their first election. Tom Bonier, the CEO of TargetSmart, a Democratic data firm, presented an analysis of Gen X voters, which has found that they are very concerned about the economy, somewhat concerned about retirement (although nowhere near as much as baby boomers), and not terribly concerned about issues like the environment or guns. A study by John Della Volpe, the director of polling at Harvard University's Kennedy School found that on economic issues, Generation Xers leaned far more to the right than any other generation. Many were attracted to Trump as an outsider and liked his policies.

Jacobs explains, "the political arc of [the] generation. Increasingly, the demographic base of the American right will be those too young to remember Watergate but too old to have spent much if any of their childhood on the Internet." It's not just their life experiences that differ from other generations. At a time when American politics is increasingly polarized around education and racial views, Generation X maintains higher rates of racial resentment than succeeding generations, according to a 2019 study by Data for Progress, while still having lower rates of educational attainment, according to a 2017 Pew Research comparison of millennials to each of the other generations.

The state of Punk 2024

It should be no surprise that Punk Culture is alive and well today and it will be tomorrow. As we have discussed, Punk is constantly transforming, evolving, changing, and adapting as cultural products become commodified in the mainstream. If it's anything, Punk is resilient. Punk continues to influence and inspire creatives across various disciplines. The DIY spirit and self-reliance continues to spawn thriving independent labels, underground venues, and grassroots communities. Punk style with its various signifiers and signs continue to symbolize individuality and resistance. Punk Culture embraces technology as a production tool in the DIY tool kit, never allowing it to overshadow creativity, authenticity, and innovation. Punk music continues to address social issues such as political corruption, economic inequality, systemic racism, and social justice. Social activism continues to foster and support resistance and solidarity. There is no doubt that in our era of political polarization, social unrest, and environmental crises, Punk Culture remains relevant.

My group has always been politically active through creative projects, activism, protesting, and voting. We share important information about candidates, particularly in our local elections where those in charge impact the quality of our daily lives. Our group is a trusted source and safe space for discussions of candidates and policies. We share the same positions on social issues.

8
Teaching Punk Culture

In the fall term of 2016, I had the opportunity to teach Punk Culture to Honors students. The timing couldn't have been better. Remember what was going on in Fall 2016? That's right, a presidential election. Who was running? Right again, Donald Trump versus Hillary Clinton. It took me back to Reagan, Jimmy Carter, and John Anderson in 1980, the first year I could vote.

Punk is political

I loved Jimmy Carter, so much so that I wore a real peanut taped on a safety pin, pinned to my blazer collar every day in ninth grade. I had lived through the daily diet of death on the news during the Vietnam War; the shooting of peaceful college protesters killed by the Ohio National Guard, known as the Kent State massacre, and the underhanded attempts to steal an election known as Watergate. And I watched as the Palestinian massacre of Israeli athletes at the 1972 Munich Olympics unfolded. These events, and the mess with British Rule in Northern Ireland, were integral in forming my political views. Carter was who he was, and though I couldn't articulate it then, I now know what I loved about him. He was authentic.

I turned 18 in August of 1980. I proudly registered to vote as an Independent. I took my responsibility to vote seriously. I was informed. I was all in for Carter until he called for a failed attempt to rescue 53 American Embassy staffers being held hostage in Iran.

It is interesting to note that all the pivotal events I have shared with you happened between 1968 and 1973. Another recent survey analyzed by Andrew Van Dam appeared in the *Washington Post* on May 24, 2024. Van Dam used YouGov to survey 2,000 American adults of 20 measures, for example, "What decade had […] the best fashion, the happiest families, the most reliable news reporting," and found no consistent pattern. Van Dam reports,

> So, we looked at the data another way, measuring the gap between each person's birth year and their ideal decade. The consistency of the resulting pattern delighted us: It shows that Americans feel nostalgia not for a specific era, but for a specific age.

That age is 11. I was 11 in 1973. I would not say the 1970s were the best decade, so I'm an outlier and I was not an average kid from an average family.

Back to my first vote. In the end, I wobbled and I voted for John Anderson. After all, I had registered as an Independent. I learned a valuable lesson from that vote and I'll never make the same mistake again. I got Reagan and he was the one I did not want, but I probably need to thank him. Punk Culture flourished while he was in power. In fact, much of our political landscape today springs from seeds sewn before and during his presidency.

I think it was the class on the evening of October 17, 2016. The topic of the evening was Sarcasm & Parody. I presented my Punk Identity piece that you read at the beginning of this book. We discussed the meaning of sarcasm and parody and the role each plays in communication. I had broken the class into groups and they were working on creating a short skit using parody, sarcasm, or both. I was doomscrolling (which it was not called back then.) through my newsfeed. I read an article that had a political pundit who either worked on campaigns or in the White House or both, who predicted a Trump win based on an experience he had had in a previous election. The cycle of that experience was being replicated in the 2016 run-up. I just knew he was right. I felt it in my gut, and where better to see that than in a room where we were exploring Punk. I didn't share this information with anyone before the election. I didn't save the article. And no matter how hard I try today, I can't find it through the search sources I have available to me. It isn't the college professor who predicts election results correctly on 13 keys, and it wasn't James Fallows in an article about the Trump/Clinton debates in *The Atlantic*.

Teaching politics through Punk

There were only three classes left post Trump's win. The second one, two weeks after the election, was a class zine-making evening. The original is literally in my hands or lap as I type. During class, each student was charged with making a two-page spread, one 8½ x 11 piece of paper that we would fold in half. After the pages were made, the group laid the pages out in the order they wanted to make the zine. We went through several rounds of rearranging the order before we settled on the sequencing and finalized the zine. I did print several copies, which I took to the 2017 PCA conference to share, but thanks to technology, we were able to make a pdf that could be shared with the student makers to use as they wish.

Some political commentary of note includes the title "We're Fucking Angry!!!!!" and pages with "WTF?" and "Fuck the System," but what is most telling is the other cultural topics, including social justice regarding police officers killing Black suspects, school debt, my body/my choice/women's rights, climate concerns, mental and physical health concerns, and wealth inequity. There are also some nonpolitical/cultural pieces that feature imagery of Punk or Punk-influenced fashion, self-care, and anti-celebrity.

The most profound statement reads as follows:

> **America** Founding through massacre & forced assimilation of Natives, mass enslavement of Africans & descendants, persecution of women without reasonable cause, backlash against immigrants […] **was** […] Segregation & rampant disparities between whites and racial minorities, classification of homosexuality as mental illness, police brutality, expanding gap between rich & poor, backlash against immigrants […] **never** […] **great**.

I am proud of the work the students did throughout the term. The zine is a great reminder to me of how education works best. Students approach a topic with an open mind, interested, ready, and willing to learn. Teachers guide them through structured materials presented through multiple lenses. Classrooms are alive with activities. Students are engaged in respectful and meaningful discussions.

Punk is a vehicle to teach critical thinking

For my entire academic career, the higher ed question has been, "How do we teach students to think critically?" My gut response was and still is "First we have to teach them to think." I could write another book about my life on the front lines of this battle that still rages on. I learned about a recently released book titled *Infusing Creative Thinking into Higher Education*, by Cyndi Burnett and John Fitzgerald Cabra. Much like Heath's *Celebrating Failure: The Power of Taking Risks, Making Mistakes, and Thinking Big*, the format is short chapters, focused on one idea, each following the same presentation format. Chapter titles include "Keep Open," "Embrace the Challenge," "Be Original," "Embracing Ambiguity," "Break Through," and "Extend the Boundaries."

There are directions on how to guide students safely through various exercises and experiences toward each goal. Frankly, I think college is kind of late to develop these skills. I've spent a lot of time thinking about where and how I learned to be a critical and creative thinker. Elizabeth detailed how her childhood journey helped her acquire the skills to think creatively. The same exposure to activities and outcomes was true for me. We've discussed how music journalism and criticism helped us become critical thinkers. Journalism and criticism were everywhere when I was a child. Philadelphia was home to two renowned newspapers of record, *The Inquirer*, which was published in the morning, and *The Evening Bulletin*, published for rush hour. We had both in my home. The evening news was another consistent source. These media outlets formed the basis for discussion in school curriculum and at home. We were encouraged to respectfully debate and discuss our thoughts and views through our school, home, and social lives.

I'm finally ready to answer the question. How do we teach students to critically think? We let them experience Punk Culture in real life. That's how.

In October of 2016, I was invited to speak to a freshman class at University of the Arts about "What Punk Can Teach Us about Innovation." In this single three-hour session, I chose to focus on anti-establishment position, DIY and activism. Students formed a band, developed a brand, wrote an activist song, and performed it with instruments made from what was at hand. While the students enjoyed the experience, the most interesting comment was made by my sage colleague, a historian, who had invited me. He posited, "Is Trump a Punk?"

It's an intriguing question, worth considering. Trump presents as antiestablishment; his communication could be likened to Punk music in terms of being fast talking, with short phrases, simplistic lyrics, with plenty of aggressive and confrontational content and posturing; and he does have a grassroots following. But as someone who has studied Trump since the 1980s, the one thing I can say for sure is that he is a narcissist, ruled by his ego, driven by personal power, filled with grievance for not being accepted by the hoi polloi, and only concerned about how things affect him and his personal identity. And that is decidedly NOT Punk.

Explore Punk Culture activities

1. Form a Band – DIY – Learn on the Fly. Iterate. Fail. Learn. Come back swinging

- Form a team or group and start a Punk band.
- Your focus is activism.
- Name your band.
- Write a song. (Short and fast rules the day.)
- Make instruments. (What that is handy can be used to make sound?)
- Style the band (What do you look like in public? How does this relate to your brand?)
- Perform your song

2. Create a zine

- Pick a Theme – Name your Zine.
- Gather your content materials – papers, magazines, posters, fliers, images, internet prints, etc.
- Grab your tools – paper, scissors, glue sticks, and sharpies.
- Create your pages – cut/paste, draw, paint, collage, write.
- Organize your pages – consider how your message(s) flow.

- Choose your cover – this should include the name of your zine and your issue's theme.
- Publish your zine – physically, digitally, or both.

3. Explore your identity

- Collect imagery that you are drawn to on- or offline from fashion, music, art, culture, album covers, books, photos, etc.
- Assemble lyrics, phrases, journals, letters, etc. that are meaningful to you.
- Grab your tools – paper, scissors, glue sticks, and sharpies.
- Create your collage that reflects your identity – cut/paste, draw, paint, collage, write.
- Reflect on how the collage connects to your identity.
- Exhibit your collage as a reminder of your identity now.

4. Perform your identity

- Review the performance "I AM ME" from the book.
- Review your Identity Collage.
- Create a live physical performance of your identity – consider words, music, movement.
- Style your performance – what will you wear when performing your identity?
- Stage your performance – what will the setting look like for your performance?
- Perform your identity – consider live, recorded, or both.

References

Allon, F. (2010). Exhibition reviews: The 80s are back. [Online] National Museum Australia. Available at: https://recollections.nma.gov.au/issues/vol_6_no_1/exhibition_reviews/the_80s_are_back [Accessed April 20, 2024].

Amorosi, A. D. (2013). *Legendary Sugar Moms bar closes suddenly in Philadelphia*. [Blog] Glamorosi Magazine. Available at: http://glamorosi.blogspot.com/2013/12/777-Legendary-Sugar-Moms-Bar-Closes-Suddenly-Philadelphia.html [Accessed April 30, 2024].

Barthes, R. (1983). *The Fashion System*. New York: Hill & Wang.

Bennett, B. R. (2019). *Neighborhood record stores*. [Blog] Philadelphia Memories. Available at: https://phillymemories.blogspot.com/2008/01/neighborhood-record-stores.html [Accessed June 1, 2024].

Berger, J. (1977). *Ways of Seeing*. 2nd ed. London: British Broadcasting Corporation.

Cave, N. (2024). *Do you miss home?* [Blog] The Red Hand Files. Available at: https://www.theredhandfiles.com/how-do-you-reconcile-this-duality/ [Accessed via email January 2024].

Cerio, M. (2015). Sugar Moms: One last drink in your favorite bar. [Entertainment/CBS Philadelphia] CBS News. Available at: https://www.cbsnews.com/philadelphia/news/sugar-moms-one-last-drink-in-your-favorite-bar/ [Accessed April 30, 2024].

Chase, T., and Van Dam, A. (2023). The most popular, obscure, Democratic, Republican & Hated Music in America, *Washington Post*, [online]. Available at: https://www.washingtonpost.com/business/2024/05/03/favorite-music-demographics/ [Accessed May 3, 2024].

"Chestnut Cabaret" (YEAR) *Wikipedia*. Available at: https://en.wikipedia.org/wiki/Chestnut_Cabaret [Accessed June 12, 2024].

Cogan, B. (2010). *The Encyclopedia of Punk Rock*. New York: Union Square & Co.

Colegrave, S., and Sullivan, C. (2005). *Punk: The Definitive Record of a Revolution*. Boston: De Capo Press.

Compass Real Estate. (2021). *Listing one-of-a-kind bi-level condominium was custom designed by Philadelphia's tattooed mom herself, Kathy Hughes*. [Online] Available at: https://www.compass.com/listing/738-pine-street-unit-b-philadelphia-pa-19106/855070628274968361/ [Accessed April 30, 2024].

Crimmins, P. (2024). Make room for cartoons among America's founding documents. [Online] WHYY. Available at: https://whyy.org/articles/political-cartoons-american-history/ [Accessed July 4, 2024]

Data for Progress. (2019). Millennials are more likely to oppose racism. [Online] Available at: https://www.dataforprogress.org/blog/2019/1/29/unpacking-millennials-racial-attitudes [Accessed June 23, 2024].

DeLuca, D. (2015). The Philadelphia Record Exchange celebrates 30 years with outdoor party. *Philadelphia Inquirer*, [online] Available at: https://www.inquirer.com/philly/entertainment/music/20150918_The_Philadelphia_Record_Exchange_celebrates_30_years_with_outdoor_party.html [Accessed June 2, 2024].

Detwiler, M. (1995). *Tribute:* The heart of rock and roll: Remembering Carol Schutzbank, 1961–1995 [Online] Hot Pot Records. Available at: https://hotpotrecords.com/about/ [Accessed May 21, 2024].

Discogs. *Bands,* Records, Labels. [Online] Available at: www.discogs.com [Accessed June 1 and 2, 2024].

Downtown West Chester. Directory, Creep Records. [Online] Available at: https://www.downtownwestchester.com/directory/creep-records/ [Accessed on June 2, 2024].

Duffty, K., and Gorman, P. (2009). *Rebel Rebel: Anti Style*. Milford, CT: Universe Publishing Company.

eBay. *Listing: J W TRECI PINK FLORAL ALOHA PRINT BARB CORE 60'S STRETCH SHIFT DRESS* [Online] Available at: https://www.ebay.com/itm/334642276122?itmmeta=01J18727T3CBH201MJF4MXJZCG&hash=item4dea3be71a:g:eMoAAOSwrZxjgYm9&itmprp=enc%3AAQAJAAAA4GE-jNTWXKWxePxcOQAPAx9d0VhGqmiRICUBjHyYkZcvuNb7B9Ra%2B2c4RPMonAU8n7eqCBFTTCpSNIxNWVIvYY5q5zfORLVBVNJ2VR686C5t38%2FSnQr9XCht9%2F06e1nDWbcZ9y6lGEsToZKJLD6cq%2Fyp4WDmiTqu%2Bv%2FVrMfQm1tG0SIiOOWgLhee4ThW%2BuaUiBRIuqVMTxwZv3Yk4ydImmSwtFrMeYg%2BMpaiGFW6EYY7N8GD3rN3bA1QkwTztx9t6pLTuub2z4e-9kyRPte14zVB8luwGQ35cR3INNIBbnkZ3G%7Ctkp%3ABk9SR5L9ileKZA [Accessed on June 25, 2024].

Erlewine, M. (2003–2020). Chestnut Cabaret PDF. [Online] Dharma Grooves. Available at: http://dharmagrooves.com/pdf/e-books/V%20CHESTNUT%20CABARET.pdf [Accessed June 2, 2024].

Fiend, E. (2017–2020). What makes Luna tick? The Book of Weirdo essay by Elizabeth Fiend aka Luna Ticks. [Online] Slaw.me. Available at: http://slaw.me/what-makes-luna-tick-the-book-of-weirdo/ [Accessed July 6, 2024]

Freedom Has No Bounds. *An archive of punk media*. [Online] Available at: https://www.freedomhasnobounds.com/zines/ [Accessed June 1, 2024].

Fulco, R., and Cogan, B. (2012). *Interview: Out of his mind: Brian Cogan and the writing of the Encyclopedia of Punk*. [Blog] RiffRaf. Available at: https://riffraf.typepad.com/riffraf/2012/07/out-of-his-mind-brian-cogan-and-the-writing-of-the-encyclopedia-of-punk.html [Accessed April 25, 2024].

Godin, S. (2008). *Tribes: We Need You to Lead Us*. New York: Portfolio.

The Great Rock 'n' Roll Swindle. (1980). [Film] UK: Julien Temple.

Greenberg, Z. (2024). The internet is over. Long live the zine. *Philadelphia Inquirer*, [online] Available at: https://www.inquirer.com/arts/philly-zines-free-library-20240504.html [Accessed June 1, 2024].

Gross, D., and Barile, N. (2020). Interview: Author Nancy Barile on her new memoir about coming of age in the '80s hardcore punk scene. [Online] No Echo. Available at: https://www.noecho.net/interviews/nancy-barile-interview [Accessed May 30, 2024].

Heath, R. (2009). *Celebrating Failure: The Power of Taking Risks, Making Mistakes, and Thinking Big*. Franklin Lakes, NJ: Career Press.

Hebdige, D. (1979). *Subculture: The Meaning of Style*. London: Routledge.

Historical Society of Pennsylvania. (2024). *Cartoons as political speech in colonial and contemporary America*. [Online] Available at: https://www.portal.hsp.org/exhibits [Accessed July 6, 2024]

Hooley, T., and Sullivan, R. (2010). *Hooleygan: Music, Mayhem, and Good Vibrations*. Belfast, Northern Ireland: Blackstaff Press.

Jacobs, B. (2022). How Gen X became the Trumpiest generation. *Politico*, [online] Available at: https://www.politico.com/news/magazine/2022/05/20/cherie-westrich-alt-rock-gen-x-maga-00033769 [Accessed May 20, 2022].

Kirk, G. (1995). *Carol L. Schutzbank – 1961–1995*. [Online] Friends of Big Shout. Available at: https://friendsofbigshout.com/carol-l-schutzbank-1961-1995/ [Accessed May 21, 2024].

LeBlanc, L. (1999). *Pretty in Punk: Girls' Gender Resistance in a Boys' Subculture*. New Brunswick, NJ: Rutgers University Press.

Library of Congress. *Chronicling America*. [Online] Available at: https://chroniclingamerica.loc.gov/ocr/ [Accessed April 27, 2024].

Marriot, H. (2024). Dressing pretty is over: This is fashion's ugly decade. *The Guardian*, [online] Available at: https://www.theguardian.com/fashion/article/2024/jun/25/ugly-fashion-trending [Accessed June 25, 2024].

MTV. (1995). *"B Side" Magazine Co-Founder Dead*. [Online] Available at: https://www.mtv.com/news/7cjh5n/b-side-magazine-co-founder-dead [Accessed May 21, 2024].

Museum of the American Revolution. (2023). *The Music of Francis Johnson: A soundtrack to Antebellum Black Philadelphia*. [Online] Available at: https://www.amrevmuseum.org/the-music-of-francis-johnson-a-soundtrack-to-antebellum-black-philadelphia [Accessed April 28, 2024].

Night Flight (Television series) (1981-1988) *Wikipedia*. Available at: https://en.wikipedia.org/wiki/New_Wave_Theatre [Accessed May 12, 2024].

Ortiz-Ospina, E., and Roser, M. (2020). *Marriages and divorces*. [Online] Our World in Data. Available at: https://ourworldindata.org/marriages-and-divorces [Accessed April 25, 2024].

PCNTV. *History of cable television and Pennsylvania's pioneers*. [Online] Available at: https://pcntv.com/pennsylvania-history-and-culture/75th-anniversary-of-cable-television/pennsylvanias-pioneers-of-cable/ [Accessed May 12, 2024].

Pew Research. (2013). *The rise of single fathers*. [Online] Available at: https://www.pewresearch.org/social-trends/2013/07/02/the-rise-of-single-fathers/ [Accessed April 25, 2024].

Pew Research. (2017). *How millennials today compare with their grandparents 50 years ago*. [Online] Available at: https://www.pewresearch.org/short-reads/2018/03/16/how-millennials-compare-with-their-grandparents/ [Accessed June 23, 2024].

Polhemus, T. (1994). *Street Style from Sidewalk to Catwalk*. London: Thames & Hudson.

Punk: Attitude. (2005). [DVD] USA: Don Letts.

"Punk rock" (YEAR) *Wikipedia*. Available at: https://en.wikipedia.org/wiki/Punk_rock [Accessed November 25, 2023].

Reynolds, S. (2006). *Rip It Up and Start Again*. New York: Penguin Books.

Sherr, S. (1996). *Big Red Rock 'n' Soul*. Philadelphia Weekly.

Silkoff, M. (2024). Teen subcultures are fading. Pity the poor kids. *New York Times*, [online] Available at: https://www.nytimes.com/2024/02/21/magazine/aesthetics-tiktok-teens.html [Accessed February 28, 2024].

Tanenbaum, M. (2022). The Trocadero aims to reopen as a revamped concert venue and restaurant, state records show. *PhillyVoice*, [online] Available at: https://www.phillyvoice.com/trocadero-theater-reopening-philly-live-music-venue-chinatown/ [Accessed June 2, 2024].

Tattooed Mom. (2024). *Now I Wanna Sniff Some Glue: An International Wheatpaste Art Show*. [Online] Available at: https://www.tattooedmomphilly.com/event/now-i-wanna-sniff-some-glue-an-international-wheatpaste-art-show/ [Accessed June 26, 2024].

Trufelman, A. (2018). *Punk Style: Articles of Interest #6*. [podcast] Articles of Interest 99%Invisible. Available at: https://99percentinvisible.org/episode/punk-style-articles-of-interest-6/ [Accessed August 14, 2022].

Walling, A., Nilsen, K., and Templeton, K. J. (2020). The Only Woman in the Room: Oral Histories of Senior Women Physicians in a Midwestern City. *Women's Health Reports*, 1(1): 279–286 [online] Available at: https://www.ncbi.nlm.nih.gov/pmc/articles/PMC7784804/ [Accessed April 25, 2024].

Weiser, C. (2008). *Broad Street*. Philadelphia: PS Books.

Wholford Boots. (2023). *The long steady history of the classic parade boot*. [Blog] Saving Soles. Available at: https://www.wohlford.ca/en-us/blogs/saving-soles/the-long-steady-history-of-the-classic-parade-boot [Accessed April 30, 2024].

Recommended further reading

1. An excellent example of Satire – *Mania* by Lionel Shriver
2. A visionary look into the future – *Snow Crash* by Neal Stephenson
3. *Mad Max* (1979)
4. *Girl in a Band: A Memoir* by Kim Gordon
5. *Punk: Attitude* – documentary

Index

Academic friends. xxii

Aerobics Instructor. 24

Aesthetics. 81

Authoritarianism. 14

Bad Brains. 76

Barile, N. 78

Barthes, R. 32, 33

Barthes' theory. 32

Belief systems. 13

Berger, J. 37

Black Flag. xiv

Bricolage and nihilism. 62

Broad Street. 51

Cabaret music. 23

Cable networks. 15

Carter, J. 89

Cartoons as Political Speech in Colonial and Contemporary America. 43

CATV system. 15

Cave, N. 12

Celebrating Failure: The Power of Taking Risks, Making Mistakes, and Thinking Big. 64

Center City entertainment scene. 24

Chase, T. 85

ChatGPT. 5

Chestnut Cabaret. 23

City Paper. 44, 77, 78

Cogan, B. 11

Colegrave, S. 13

Comics. 44

Community activism. xi

Corporate messaging. 37–39

Creem magazine. 12, 40

Creep Records. 30

Crimmins, P. 43

Crumm, R. 44

Dam, V. 90

Data for Progress. 87

Declaration of Independence. 26

DeLuca, D. 30

Detwiler, M. 77

Dictionary.com. xvi

Digital media. 81, 84

Discogs.com. 50

DIY spaces. 17

Downtown West Chester Directory. 30
Drexel Institute of Technology. 21
Duffty, K. 33

E Morto Cosi. 52
eBay. 67
Empowerment. xi
Encyclopedia of Punk, The. 11
Environmentalism. 74
Erlewine, M. 24
Exhibit Design. 3

Fanzines. 40, 41, 79
Fashion designers. 38
Fashion magazines. 15, 32
Fashion merchandising. 1
Fashion System, The. 32
Fiend, E. 44, 65; Big Tea Party years. 71; family. 68; garment. 74; journey to Punk. 70; Mummer's Parade. 72, 73; music. 67; nonconventional methods. 70; old-school punk. 67; personal style. 68; Punk ideology. 74; Tea Party movement. 71
Flag of Democracy. 21
Flash Glass. 61
Free Library of Philadelphia, The. 42
Freedom has no bounds website. 41

Ganoshowanna. 21
Girl band. 53
Global audience. 16
Godin, S. 7
Good Friday Agreement. 5
Gothic Lolitas. 4
Great Rock 'n' Roll Swindle, The. 9–11
Greenberg, Z. 41
Gross, D. 78

Haegele, K. 42
Health. xi, 74, 78
Heath, R. 7
Hebdige, D. 6
Historic; buildings. 26; homes. 22; institutions. 29; Old City. 26; references. 2
Historical Society of Pennsylvania (HSP). 43
Holmstrom, J. 12
Hooters, The. 24
HSP. *See* Historical Society of Pennsylvania (HSP)
Hughes, John. 25

Industrial spaces. 26

Jacobs, B. 85, 86
Jeff Jenkins' basement. 17, 20
Johnson, F. 48
Jove, D. 15

KeN. 51, 52, 53, 54
Kent State Massacre. 89

LeBlanc, L. xv, 6, 19
Letts, D. 69
Lifestyle obligations. 82
Lindy Center for Civic Engagement. 22
Love Club, The. 29

Maclaren, M. 9
"Make Room for Cartoons among America's Founding Documents." 43
Marriot, H. 82
Marsh, D. 12
Masculine aggression. xv
Mass media. 10
Maximumrocknroll. 41
McNeil, L. 12
Mental health. 92
MissionCreep. 44
MTV. 10, 15, 77
Mummer's Parade. 72, 73
Museum of the American Revolution. 47
Music criticism. 39
Music magazines. 40

National audience. 16

Night Flight. 15
Non-digital communication. 14

Olio. 78
Original punks. xv
Outsiders. xxi, 33

Partisan politics. 43
Performative approach. 13
Pew Research. 87
Philadelphia Memories Blog. 29
Philadelphia Record Exchange. 30
Philadelphia underground rock scene. 77
Philly Punk scene. xxii, 51, 58, 65, 75, 84
Philly Punk style. 32
Philly Soul. 48
Physical health. 92
Polhemus, T. 1
Political cartoons. 43
Pop music. 60
Popular Culture Association. 3
Pre-digital. 42
Pretenders, The. 23
Pretty in Punk: Girl's Gender Resistance in a Boy's Subculture. 6
Pre-video. 16
Publicity image. 37

Punk Culture; content production. 83; create zine. 95, 96; DIY. 95; explore identity. 96; fashion. 34, 36, 38, 39; global prespective. 4; lifestyle. 14; music. 11; PCA. 4; perform identity. 96; political. 89, 90, 91; technology. 87; women's roles. xi

Punk music; Brian's book. 11; live. 67; musicians. 85; Philadelphia. 31; post. 63; Sex Pistols. 10; social issues. 87; USA. 10

Punk rock. xiv, xv, 12, 28, 52, 78

Punk style; biker. 35; British. 10; combat boots. 34; jeans. , ; leather jacket. 58, 59; local. 32; London. ; rebel style. 33; T-shirt. 34; thrift shop clothing. 35; tribes clothing. 36; unisex look. 32; women's look. 33

Punk Style, Articles of Interest #6. 10

Punk: the Definitive Record of a Revolution. 13

Punk: Attitude. xiv

Punks; Australian. 13; childhood. xviii, xix; common threads. 79; creative work. 60, 61; critical thinking. 93; cultural products. 14; definition. 14; digital world. 83; DIY spaces. 17; local bands. 49, 50; local group. 21; media. 39; national media. 40; New Wave bands. 15; origin. 12; original. xv; PCA. 3; Philly spaces. 17; pre-2000. 6; street style. 3; subcultures. 80, 82; teaching politics. 91, 92; tribes. 7; UK/US. 13; women. 54; zines. 40

Ramones, The. 23, 63, 85

Rebel Rebel Anti-Style. 33

Record stores. 29, 30, 31

Reverse engineering. 2

Revolutionary politics. 43

Reynolds, S. 63

Rhode Island School of Design (RISD). 58

Rip It Up and Start Again. 63

Rock genre. 30

Rocky Horror Picture Show. 27

Ruby Tuesday. xv

Schaechter, J. 35, 44, 51, 54; bricolage and nihilism. 62; creative work. 60; first leather jacket. 58; process. 61, 62; second leather jacket. 59; third leather jacket. 59; *vs.* Revelogic. 60

Serial Killers album. 24

Service economy. 20

Sex Pistols. 9, 10, 63

She Males, The. 28

Sherr, S. 50

Silkoff, M. 81

SmartLynx. 84

Soapbox. 42

Social media. 19, 71

Societal norms. 13

Sound of Philadelphia, The. 49

South Street. 27

Spiritual Cramp. 30, 31

Stained Glass Window. 61

Stereotypical Punk style. xv

Stick Men house. 77

Style Tribes. 3

Subcultural styles. 1, 2

Subculture: The Meaning of Style. 6

Sullivan, C. 13

Tattooed Mom. 75, 76

Teaching methodology. 3

Temple University's Special Collections and Research Center. 42

Theater of the Living Arts (TLA). 27, 28

Thrifting. 38

Transatlantic commerce. 43

Tristate area. 17

Troc, The. 25

Trocadero, The. 25, 27

Trouser Press magazine. 40

Underground Arts. 31

Underground Philly music scene. 19

"Video Killed the Radio Star." 16

Visual merchandising (VM). 2, 3

Weiser, C. 51

West Side Club. 17, 18

Wilkinson, S. 43

Young Americans album. 48

Zines. 40, 42

www.ingramcontent.com/pod-product-compliance
Lightning Source LLC
Chambersburg PA
CBHW060838190426
43197CB00040B/2675